p

g

t

alues

900

to

nt

ermous

ermous

COLLECTOR BOOKS
A Division of Schroeder Publishing Co., Inc.

The current values in this book should be used only as guide. They are not intended to set prices, which vary from one section of the country to another. Auction prices as well as dealer prices vary greatly and are affected by condition as well as demand. Neither the Author nor the Publisher assumes responsibility for any losses that might be incurred as a result of consulting this guide.

Seaching for a Publisher?
We are always looking for knowledgeable people considered experts within their fields. If you feel there is a real need for a book on your collectible subject and have a large comprehensive collection, contact us.

COLLECTOR BOOKS
P.O. Box 3009
Paducah, Kentucky 42002-3009

Introduction

This is an identification and value guide. Very little in the way of instruction and directions should be required to use a value guide but some words of explanation might be in order.

First of all the suggested values are just that. They are not the final word on an item's absolute worth. That figure can only be determined by the buyer's willingness to purchase and the seller's ability to hold to an asking price. But the values found in this book should be a reasonable guide of what certain firearms are selling for on average around the country.

Geography plays an important part in establishing value. Some guns are more in demand in particular locales than other firearms that are equal in rarity, workmanship and quantities. There are also guns that have a good resale value just because they are manufactured by a particular company. Maybe the company's track record for producing high quality firearms is especially good. Or, maybe there is just an aura of greatness that has been associated with the manufacturer for one reason or another.

Condition is also important in establishing a value. The values in this guide relate to firearms in very good to excellent condidion. That is: in good working condition with no appreciable wear on working surfaces, no corrosion or pitting with only minor surface dents or scratches at one end of the spectrum to: in new condition, used very little, with no noticeable marring of the wood or metal and with perfect bluing except at the muzzle or on sharp edges.

The value range should be a reasonable guide to the gun's real selling worth. But readers who disagree with the pricing structure are encouraged to do further research to ascertain what they consider to be the value.

The illustrations in this guide are from gun companies' promotional materials and as such are not meant to be representative of size relation.

There is no way that a book of this size can be all inclusive of the firearms made in the world but we hope it is a good survey of most of the firearms that are readily available on the open market.

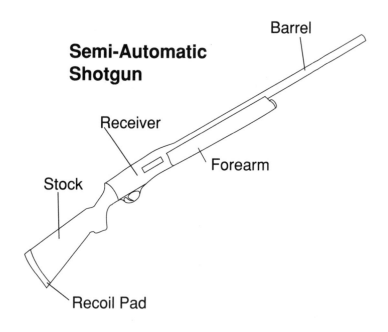

Semi-Automatic Shotgun

Barrel

Receiver

Forearm

Stock

Recoil Pad

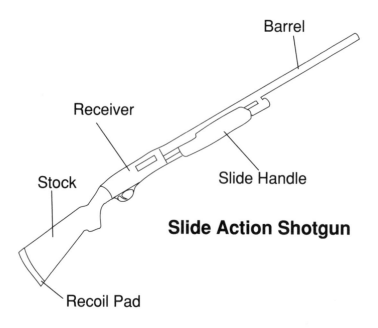

Barrel

Receiver

Slide Handle

Stock

Slide Action Shotgun

Recoil Pad

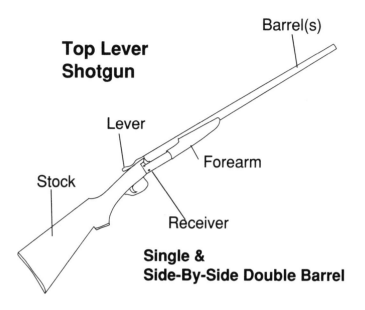

Top Lever Shotgun

Barrel(s)

Lever

Forearm

Stock

Receiver

Single & Side-By-Side Double Barrel

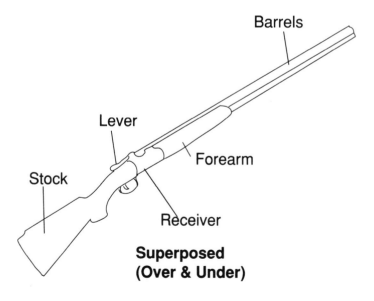

Barrels

Lever

Forearm

Stock

Receiver

Superposed (Over & Under)

Acknowledgments

The companies included for the use of catalogs, advertisements and promotional material.

A special thanks to the following gun manufacturers for additional photos, information and assistance: Beretta Arms Co., Inc., Browning, Commercial Trading Imports, Inc. for material on Baikal shotguns, Harrington & Richardson, Inc., Ithaca Gun Co., Mannlicher, Marlin for material on Marlin and Marlin-Glenfield, O.F. Mossberg & Sons, Inc. for material on Mossberg and New Haven shotguns, Remington, Richland Arms Co., Savage Arms for material on Savage shotguns, Stevens shotguns, and Fox shotguns, Sears, Roebuck & Co., for material on Sears shotguns and Ted Williams shotguns; Smith & Wesson, Weatherby, Inc., Winchester-Western for material on Winchester shotguns, and U.S. Repeating Arms for material on Winchester shotguns.

Petersen Publishing Company for the use of photographs from *Guns and Ammo Annual*, 1977, 1982 and *Hunting Annual* 1983.

Russell Scheffer of Scheffer Studio for graphic arrangement of the material. Russell is always there, day or night, to crank out an amazing amount of work on extremely short notice.

The crew that makes up the editorial staff of Collector Books. Their dedication and hard work make an unbelievable number of books on antiques and collectibles indispensible tools for collectors everywhere.

Contents

AYA

AYA Matador
Gauge: 10, 12, 16, 20, 20 magnum
Action: Box lock; top lever break-open; hammerless; selective single trigger & automatic ejector
Magazine: None
Barrel: Double barrel, 26", 28", or 30" any choke combination
Finish: Blued; checkered walnut pistol grip stock & beavertail forearm
Estimated Value: $360.00 - $450.00

AYA Matador II
Same as the Matador except: ventilated rib
Estimated Value: $400.00 - $500.00

AYA Bolero
Same as the Matador except: non-selective single trigger & extractors; 28 & 410 gauges
Estimated Value: $310.00 - $390.00

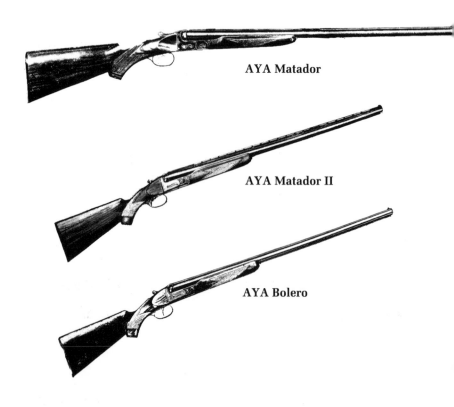

AYA Matador

AYA Matador II

AYA Bolero

Armalite

Armalite AR-17

Armalite AR-17
Gauge: 12
Action: Semi-automatic; gas operated; hammerless
Magazine: 2-shot
Barrel: 24" aluminum alloy; interchangeable choke tubes
Finish: Gold anodized or black anodized; plastic stock & forearm
Estimated Value: $500.00 - $675.00

Baikal

Baikal Model IJK-27 and IJK-27EIC
Gauge: 12 or 20
Action: Box lock; top lever break-open; hammerless; selective single trigger; IJK-27EIC has selective ejectors, add $40.00 for IJK-27EIC
Magazine: None
Barrel: Over & under double barrel; 26", 28", or 30" improved cylinder & modified or modified & full chokes; ventilated rib
Finish: Blued; engraved receiver; hand checkered walnut pistol grip stock & forearm
Estimated Value: $240.00 - $300.00

Baikal Model IJK-27EIC Silver
Same as the Model IJK-27EIC except: silver inlays and fancy engraving
Estimated Value: $395.00 - $495.00

Baikal Model IJK-12
Similar to the IJK-27 except: no engraving; no recoil pad; 28" barrel only
Estimated Value: $200.00 - $250.00

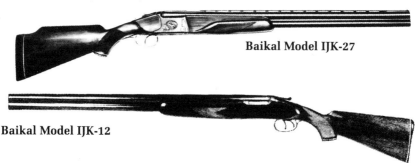

Baikal Model IJK-27

Baikal Model IJK-12

Baikal

Baikal TOZ-66

Baikal TOZ-66
Gauge: 12
Action: Box lock; top lever break-open; exposed hammers
Magazine: None
Barrel: Double barrel (side by side); 28" chrome lined barrels; variety of chokes
Finish: Blued; checkered wood pistol grip stock & short tapered forearm; engraving
Estimated Value: $205.00 - $260.00

Baikal Model TOZ-34E Souvenir
Gauge: 12, 20, or 28
Action: Box lock; top lever break-open; hammerless; selective ejectors and cocking indicators
Magazine: None
Barrel: Over and under double barrel; 26" or 28" improved cylinder & modified or modified & full; ventilated rib on 12 and 20 gauge; solid rib on 28 gauge
Finish: Blued; select walnut, hand checkered pistol grip stock and forearm; engraved receiver
Estimated Value: $450.00 - $600.00

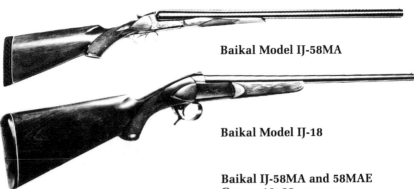

Baikal Model IJ-58MA

Baikal Model IJ-18

Baikal Model IJ-18
Gauge: 12, or 20
Action: Box lock; top lever break-open; hammerless; single shot; cocking indicator
Magazine: None
Barrel: 26", 28" modified, or 30" full choke
Finish: Blued; checkered walnut-stained hardwood pistol grip stock and tapered forearm; engraved receiver
Estimated Value: $60.00 - $70.00

Baikal IJ-58MA and 58MAE
Gauge: 12, 20 magnum
Action: Box lock; top lever break-open; hammerless
Magazine: None
Barrel: Double barrel (side by side); 26" improved cylinder & modified; 28" modified & full chokes; chrome lined
Finish: Blued; checkered walnut pistol grip stock and short tapered forearm; engraved receiver; IJ-58MAE has selective ejectors; add $28.00 for IJ-58MAE
Estimated Value: $220.00 - $275.00

Baikal Model MC-8
Gauge: 12
Action: Box lock; top lever break-open; hammerless
Magazine: None
Barrel: Over and under double barrel; trap, skeet; 26" or 28" modified or full chokes; chrome lined barrels
Finish: Blued; checkered walnut Monte Carlo pistol grip stock and forearm; engraved receiver
Estimated Value: $1,300.00 - $1,800.00

Baikal Model MC-21
Gauge: 12
Action: Semi-auto; hammerless; side ejection
Magazine: 5-shot tubular
Barrel: 26" improved cylinder; 28" modified; 30" full chokes; ventilated rib
Finish: Blued; checkered walnut pistol grip stock and forearm; engraved receiver
Estimated Value: $250.00 - $325.00

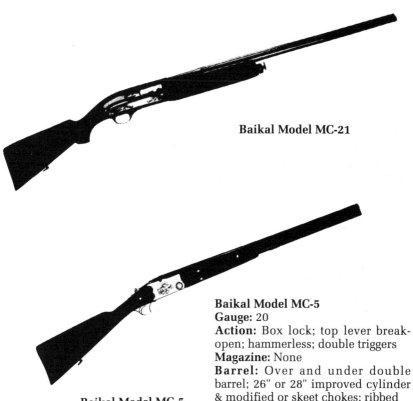

Baikal Model MC-21

Baikal Model MC-5

Baikal Model MC-5
Gauge: 20
Action: Box lock; top lever break-open; hammerless; double triggers
Magazine: None
Barrel: Over and under double barrel; 26" or 28" improved cylinder & modified or skeet chokes; ribbed
Finish: Blued; checkered walnut pistol grip or straight stock and forearm; engraved receiver
Estimated Value: $650.00 - $850.00

Baker

Baker Batavia Leader

Baker Black Beauty Special
Similar to Baker Batavia Leader
except: higher quality wood and
finish; engraved; add $75.00 for
automatic extractors
Estimated Value: $500.00 - $675.00

Baker Black Beauty Special

Baker Batavia Leader
Gauge: 12, 16, or 20
Action: Box lock; top lever break-
Open; hammerless; add $75.00 for
automatic extractors
Magazine: None
Barrel: 26", 28", 30", or 32" double
barrel (side by side); any standard
choke combination
Finish: Blued; walnut pistol grip
stock and forearm.
Estimated Value: $360.00 - $450.00

Beretta

Beretta Companion FS-1

Beretta Companion FS-1
Gauge: 12, 16, 20, 28, or 410
Action: Underlever break-open;
hammerless; single shot; folding
shot gun
Magazine: None
Barrel: 26" or 28" full choke
Finish: Blued; checkered walnut
pistol grip stock and forearm
Estimated Value: $100.00 - $130.00

Beretta Model 412
Gauge: 12, 20, 28, or 410
Action: Underlever, break-open;
hammerless; single shot
Magazine: None
Barrel: 28" full or modified choke
Finish: Blued; checkered walnut
semi-pistol grip stock and forearm
Estimated Value: $130.00 - $160.00

Beretta Mark II Trap
Gauge: 12
Action: Box lock; top lever break-open; hammerless; single shot
Magazine: None
Barrel: 32" or 34" full choke; ventilated rib
Finish: Blued; checkered walnut Monte Carlo pistol grip stock and forearm; recoil pad; engraving
Estimated Value: $420.00 - $525.00

Beretta Mark II Trap

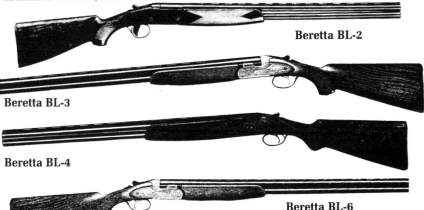

Beretta BL-2

Beretta BL-3

Beretta BL-4

Beretta BL-6

Beretta BL-1
Gauge: 12
Action: Box lock; top lever break-open; hammerless; double triggers
Magazine: None
Barrel: Over and under double barrel; chrome steel; 26" or 30" improved cylinder & modified or modified & full chokes
Finish: Blued; checkered walnut semi-pistol grip stock and forearm
Estimated Value: $365.00 - $460.00

Beretta BL-2
Similar to the BL-1 except: selective single trigger
Estimated Value: $415.00 - $520.00

Beretta BL-3
Similar to the BL-2 except: ventilated rib; engraving
Estimated Value: $520.00 - $650.00

Beretta BL-4 and BL-5
Similar to the BL-3 except: deluxe engraving and checkering; automatic ejectors; add $200.00 for BL-5
Estimated Value: $600.00 - $750.00

Beretta BL-6
The finest of the BL line; highest quality checkering and engraving; automatic ejectors
Estimated Value: $1,050.00 - $1,300.00

Beretta

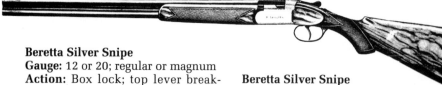

Beretta Silver Snipe
Gauge: 12 or 20; regular or magnum
Action: Box lock; top lever break-open; hammerless; add $25.00 for single selective trigger
Magazine: None
Barrel: 26"or 30"; ribbed; over and under double barrel; improved cylinder & modified; modified & full; full or skeet chokes
Finish: Blued; nickel receiver; checkered walnut pistol grip stock and forearm
Estimated Value: $440.00 - $550.00

Beretta Golden Snipe
Similar to the Silver Snipe except: ventilated rib; automatic ejectors
Estimated Value: $560.00 - $700.00

Beretta Silver Snipe

Beretta Asel
Gauge: 12 or 20
Action: Box lock; top lever break-open; hammerless; automatic ejectors; single trigger
Magazine: None
Barrel: Over and under double barrel; 25", 28", or 30" improved cylinder & modified or modified & full chokes
Finish: Blued; checkered walnut semi-pistol grip stock and forearm
Estimated Value: $1,050.00 - $1,325.00

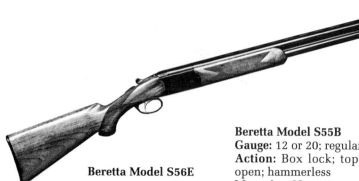

Beretta Model S56E

Beretta Model S56E
Similar to Model S55B except; scroll engraving on the receiver; selective automatic ejectors
Estimated Value: $640.00 - $800.00

Beretta Model S55B
Gauge: 12 or 20; regular or magnum
Action: Box lock; top lever break-open; hammerless
Magazine: None
Barrel: Over and under double barrel; chrome lined; ventilated rib; 26" improved cylinder & modified; 28" or 30" modified & full; 30" full in 12 gauge
Finish: Blued; checkered walnut pistol grip stock and beavertail forearm; recoil pad on magnum
Estimated Value: $570.00 - $710.00

Beretta Model 680 Trap

**Beretta Model 680
Competition Skeet**
Gauge: 12
Action: Top lever, break-open; hammerless; automatic ejectors; single selective trigger
Magazine: None
Barrel: Over and under double barrel; 26" or 28" skeet choke barrels; ventilated rib
Finish: Blued; checkered walnut pistol grip stock and forearm; silver gray receiver with engraving; goldplated trigger
Estimated Value: $1,050.00 - $1,320.00

Beretta Model 680 Trap
Similar to the Model 680 Skeet except: Monte Carlo stock recoil pad; 30" or 32" improved modified & full choke barrels
Estimated Value: $1,060.00 - $1,330.00

Beretta Model 680 Mono Trap
Similar to the Model 680 Trap except: single barrel with a high ventilated rib; 32" or 34" full choke barrel
Estimated Value: $1,075.00 - $1,340.00

Beretta Model 685

Beretta Model 625
Gauge: 12 or 20; regular or magnum
Action: Box lock; top lever break-open; hammerless
Magazine: None
Barrel: 26" improved cylinder & modified; 28" or 30" modified & full; double barrel (side by side)
Finish: Blued; gray receiver; checkered walnut pistol grip or straight stock and tapered forearm
Estimated Value: $660.00 - $825.00

Beretta Model 626; 626 Onyx
Similar to the Model 625 except: selective automatic ejectors; deduct 30% for Model 626
Estimated Value: $1,125.00 - $1,400.00

Beretta Model 627EL, 627EELL
Similar to the Model 626 except: higher grade finish and engraved sideplate; add 70% for EELL Model
Estimated Value: $1,960.00 - $2,450.00

Beretta Model 685
Gauge: 12 or 20; regular or magnum
Action: Top lever, break-open; hammerless; single selective trigger
Magazine: None
Barrel: Over and under double barrel; 26" improved cylinder & modified, 28" or 30" modified & full, 30" full & full; ventilated rib
Finish: Blued; checkered walnut pistol grip stock and fluted forearm; silver gray receiver with light engraving
Estimated Value: $620.00 - $775.00

Pocket Guide to Shotguns

Beretta

Beretta Model 687EELL

Beretta Model 686
Gauge: 12 or 20; regular or magnum
Action: Top lever, break-open; hammerless; single selective trigger; selective automatic ejectors
Magazine: None
Barrel: Over and under double barrel; 26" improved cylinder & modified; 28" or 30" modified & full; 30" full & full; ventilated rib; multi-choke tubes available
Finish: Blued; checkered walnut pistol grip stock and fluted forearm; silver gray receiver with engraving; recoil pad on magnum; add 12% for Ultralight Onyx model; add 44% for Sporting Clays model
Estimated Value: $820.00 - $1,020.00

Beretta Model 687L
Gauge: 12 or 20; regular or magnum
Action: Top lever, break-open; hammerless; selective automatic ejectors; single selective trigger
Magazine: None
Barrel: Over and under double barrel; 26" or 28" with interchangeable choke tubes; ventilated rib
Finish: Blued; grayed receiver with engraving; checkered walnut pistol grip stock and forearm; add 25% for Golden Onyx model; add 38% for Sporting Clays model
Estimated Value: $945.00 - $1,180.00

Beretta Model 687EL, 687 EELL
Similar to the Model 687L except: higher quality finish, extensive engraving on receiver and sideplates; add 50% for EELL Model
Estimated Value: $1,910.00 - $2,385.00

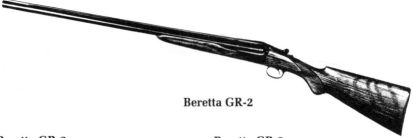

Beretta GR-2

Beretta GR-2
Gauge: 12 or 20
Action: Box lock, top lever, break-open; hammerless
Magazine: None
Barrel: Double barrel (side by side); 26" or 30"; variety of choke combinations
Finish: Blued; checkered walnut semi-pistol grip stock and forearm
Estimated Value: $450.00 - $570.00

Beretta GR-3
Similar to the GR-2 except: single selective trigger
Estimated Value: $500.00 - $625.00

Beretta GR-4
Similar to the GR-3 except: automatic ejectors; engraving and deluxe wood
Estimated Value: $610.00 - $760.00

Pocket Guide to Shotguns

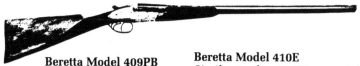

Beretta Model 409PB

Beretta Model 409PB
Gauge: 12, 16, 20, or 28
Action: Box lock, top lever, break-open; hammerless; double triggers
Magazine: None
Barrel: Double barrel (side by side); 27½", 28½", or 30"; improved cylinder & modified or modified & full chokes
Finish: Blued; checkered walnut straight or pistol grip stock and small tapered forearm; engraved
Estimated Value: $520.00 - $650.00

Beretta Model 410E
Similar to the 409PB except: higher quality finish and engraving; automatic ejectors
Estimated Value: $660.00 - $820.00

Beretta Model 411E
Similar to 410E except: higher quality finish & engraving
Estimated Value: $880.00 - $1,100.00

Beretta Model 410E

Beretta Model 410

Beretta Model 424

Beretta Model 424
Gauge: 12 or 20
Action: Box lock; top lever, break-open; hammerless; double trigger
Magazine: None
Barrel: Double barrel (side by side); chrome lined; matted rib; 26" or 28" improved cylinder & modified or modified & full chokes
Finish: Blued; checkered walnut straight grip stock and forearm
Estimated Value: $630.00 - $790.00

Beretta Model 410
Gauge: 10 magnum
Action: Box lock; top lever, break-open; hammerless; double triggers
Magazine: None
Barrel: Double barrel (side by side); 27½", 28½", or 30"; improved cylinder & modified or modified & full chokes
Finish: Blued; checkered walnut pistol stock & short tapered forearm
Estimated Value: $860.00 - $1,075.00

Beretta

Beretta Silver Hawk Featherweight

Beretta Model 426
Gauge: 12 or 20; magnum
Action: Top lever, break-open; hammerless; single selective trigger; selective automatic ejectors
Magazine: None
Barrel: Double barrel (side by side); 26" improved cylinder & modified or 28" modified & full; solid rib
Finish: Blued; checkered walnut pistol grip stock and tapered forearm; silver gray engraved receiver; silver pigeon inlaid
Estimated Value: $800.00 - $1,000.00

Beretta Silver Hawk Featherweight
Gauge: 12, 16, 20, or 28
Action: Box lock; top lever, break-open; hammerless
Magazine: None
Barrel: Double barrel (side by side); 26" or 32"; variety of chokes; matted rib
Finish: Blued; checkered walnut pistol grip stock and forearm
Estimated Value: $460.00 - $575.00

Beretta Silver Hawk Featherweight Magnum
Similar to the Silver Hawk Featherweight except: 10 or 12 gauge magnum; chrome lined 30" or 32" barrels; ventilated rib; recoil pad
Estimated Value: $520.00 - $650.00

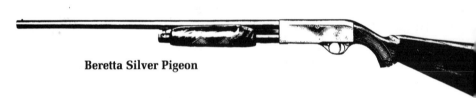

Beretta Silver Pigeon

Beretta Silver Pigeon
Gauge: 12
Action: Slide action; hammerless
Magazine: 5-shot tubular
Barrel: 26" or 32"; various chokes
Finish: Blued; engraved and inlaid with silver pigeon; chrome trigger; checkered walnut pistol grip stock and slide handle
Estimated Value: $260.00 - $325.00

Beretta Gold Pigeon
Similar to the Silver Pigeon except: heavier engraving; gold pigeon inlaid; ventilated rib; gold trigger
Estimated Value: $550.00 - $690.00

Beretta Ruby Pigeon
Similar to the Gold Pigeon except: deluxe engraving; inlaided pigeon has ruby eye
Estimated Value: $635.00 - $795.00

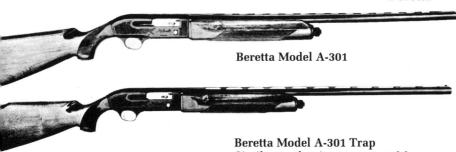

Beretta Model A-301

Beretta Model A-301 Trap

Beretta Model A-301
Gauge: 12 or 20; regular or magnum; add $45.00 for magnum
Action: Gas operated, semi-automatic; hammerless
Magazine: 3-shot tubular
Barrel: 26" improved cylinder; 28" modified or full; 30" full in 12 gauge; ventilated rib; chrome molydenum
Finish: Blued; checkered walnut pistol grip stock and forearm; decorated alloy receiver; recoil pad on magnum model
Estimated Value: $320.00 - $400.00

Beretta Model A-301 Trap
Similar to the A-301 except: Monte Carlo stock, recoil pad & gold plated trigger; 12 gauge only; 30" full choke
Estimated Value: $345.00 - $430.00

Beretta Model A-301 Skeet
Similar to the A-301 Trap except: 26" skeet choke barrel
Estimated Value: $340.00 - $425.00

Beretta Model A-301 Deer Gun
Similar to the A-301 except: 22" slug barrel; adjustable open sights
Estimated Value: $325.00 - $410.00

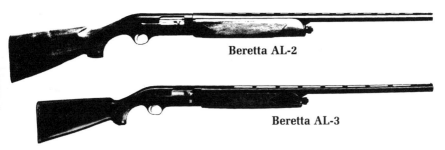

Beretta AL-2

Beretta AL-3

Beretta AL-1
Gauge: 12 or 20; regular or magnum
Action: Gas operated, semi-automatic; hammerless
Magazine: 3-shot tubular
Barrel: 26" or 30"; improved cylinder, modified full or skeet, chokes; ventilated rib
Finish: Blued; checkered walnut pistol grip stock and forearm
Estimated Value: $260.00 - $325.00

Beretta AL-3
Similar to the AL-2 except: light engraving
Estimated Value: $300.00 - $380.00

Beretta AL-2
Similar to the AL-1 except: ventilated rib; recoil pad; chrome lined bore
Estimated Value: $290.00 - $360.00

Beretta

Beretta Silver Lark
Gauge: 12
Action: Gas operated, semi-automatic; hammerless
Magazine: 5-shot tubular
Barrel: 26"-32", improved cylinder, modified or full chokes
Finish: Blued; checkered walnut pistol grip stock and forearm
Estimated Value: $265.00 - $330.00

Beretta Gold Lark
Similar to the Silver Lark with high-quality engraving and ventilated rib
Estimated Value: $360.00 - $450.00

Beretta Ruby Lark
Similar to the Silver Lark with deluxe engraving and a stainless steel barrel
Estimated Value: $480.00 - $600.00

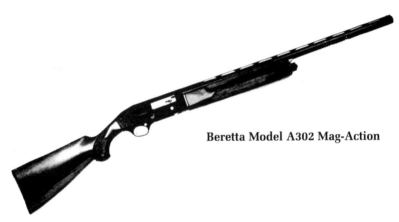

Beretta Model A302 Mag-Action

Beretta Model A302 Skeet
Similar to the Model A302 Mag-Action except: 26" skeet choke barrel
Estimated Value: $400.00 - $500.00

Beretta Model A302 Mag-Action
Gauge: 12 or 20; regular or magnum
Action: Gas operated, semi-automatic
Magazine: 3-shot tubular
Barrel: 26" improved cylinder; 28" modified or full; 30" full choke; or changable choke tubes; ventilated rib; add 5% for multi-choke model with four choke tubes
Finish: Blued; checkered walnut pistol grip stock and fluted forearm
Estimated Value: $380.00 - $475.00

Beretta Model A302 Trap
Similar to the Model A302 Mag-Action except: Monte Carlo stock & 30" full choke barrel
Estimated Value: $400.00 - $510.00

Beretta Model A302 Slug
Similar to the Model A302 Mag-Action except: 22" slug barrel; adjustable front sight, folding leaf rear sight; swivels
Estimated Value: $390.00 - $490.00

Pocket Guide to Shotguns

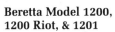

Beretta Model 1200F

**Beretta Model 1200,
1200 Riot, & 1201**
Gauge: 12 regular or magnum
Action: Gas operated, semi-automatic
Magazine: 3-shot tubular; 7-shot in riot model
Barrel: 24", 26", or 28" modified, full, or changeable choke tubes; 20" cylinder bore on Riot Model; add 5% for Riot Model
Finish: Blued, non-glare; synthetic stock & forearm
Estimated Value: $375.00 - $470.00

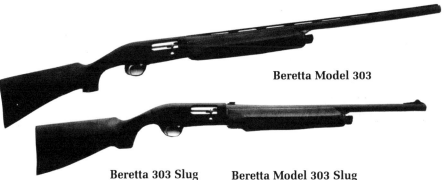

Beretta Model 303

Beretta 303 Slug

Beretta Model 303 Slug
Similar to the Model 303 except: 22" cylinder bore barrel, with rifle sights
Estimated Value: $415.00 - $520.00

Beretta Model 303
Gauge: 12 or 20; regular or magnum
Action: Gas operated, semi-automatic
Magazine: 2-shot plugged tubular
Barrel: 26", 28", 30", or 32" in a variety of chokes or interchangeable choke tubes; deduct 6% for guns without interchangeable choke tubes; 24" barrel on youth model
Finish: Blued; checkered walnut pistol grip stock & forearm; recoil pad on youth model; add 14% for Sporting Clays Model
Estimated Value: $440.00 - $550.00

Beretta Model 303 Skeet
Similar to the Model 303 except: 26" skeet choke barrel
Estimated Value: $440.00 - $550.00

Beretta Model 303 Trap
Similar to the Model 303 except: 30" or 32" full choke barrel or interchangeable choke tubes; add 6% for set interchangeable choke tubes
Estimated Value: $440.00 - $550.00

Beretta Model A 390 ST
Gauge: 12, regular or magnum
Action: Gas operated, semi-automatic; a self-compensating gas operating system performs with any 12 gauge factory load
Magazine: 3-shot tubular
Barrel: 24", 26", 28", or 30" with mobilchoke screw-in choke tubes; ventilated rib
Finish: Black; checkered walnut pistol grip stock & forearm; a new stock drop system and cast-off spacer allows for stock adjustment
Estimated Value: $470.00 - $585.00

Beretta Model A 390 ST Slug
Same as Model A 390 ST except: 20" or 22" barrel; fixed choke; plain barrel with hook-in bases for scope mounting; blade front sight and adjustable rear
Estimated Value: $440.00 - $550.00

Beretta Model A 304 Ultralight
Similar to the Model A 390 except: 12 gauge 2¾ only; doesn't use the self compensating gas system
Estimated Value: $440.00 - $550.00

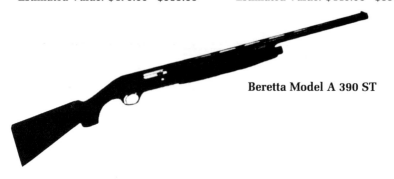

Beretta Model A 390 ST

Bernardelli

Bernardelli Roma
Gauge: 12, 16, 20, or 28
Action: Anson & Deeley type; top lever break-open; hammerless; double trigger; automatic ejector
Magazine: None
Barrel: Double barrel; 27½" or 29½" modified & full choke
Finish: Blued; checkered walnut straight or pistol grip stock & forearm; produced in three grades; add $50.00 for single trigger
Estimated Value:
    Roma 3: $650.00 - $800.00
    Roma 4: $750.00 - $1,000.00
    Roma 5: $825.00 - $1,025.00

Bernardelli Roma

Bernardelli Game Cock
Gauge: 12 or 20
Action: Box lock; top lever break-open; double trigger; hammerless
Magazine: None
Barrel: Double barrel; 25" improved & modified or 28" modified & full chokes
Finish: Blued; checkered walnut straight stock & forearm; light engraving
Estimated Value: $600.00 - $750.00

Bernardelli Game Cock Deluxe
Same as the Game Cock with light scroll engraving; single trigger; automatic ejectors
Estimated Value: $640.00 - $800.00

Bernardelli Game Cock Premier
Same as the Game Cock with more engraving; selective single trigger; automatic ejectors
Estimated Value: $760.00 - $950.00

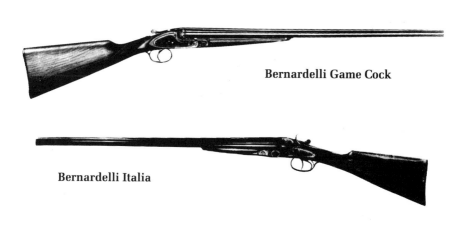

Bernardelli Game Cock

Bernardelli Italia

Bernardelli Italia
Gauge: 12, 16, or 20
Action: Top lever break-open; exposed hammer; double trigger
Magazine: None
Barrel: Double barrel; chrome lined 30" modified & full chokes
Finish: Blued; engraved receiver; checkered walnut straight grip stock & forearm
Estimated Value: $850.00 - $1,065.00

Bernardelli Brescia

Bernardelli Brescia
Same as the Italia except: 28" barrels; 26" barrels in 20 gauge; modified & improved cylinder bore
Estimated Value: $600.00 - $800.00

Bernardelli/Breda

Bernardelli Holland

Bernardelli Holland

Bernardelli Holland
Gauge: 12
Action: top lever break-open; hammerless; double trigger; automatic ejectors
Magazine: None
Barrel: Double barrel, 26" to 32" any choke combination
Finish: Blued; straight or pistol grip stock & forearm; engraving
Estimated Value: $1,500.00 - $2,000.00

Bernardelli Holland Deluxe

Bernardelli Holland Deluxe
Same as the Holland with engraved hunting scene
Estimated Value: $1,900.00 - $2,500.00

Bernardelli St. Uberto
Gauge: 12, 16, 20, or 28
Action: Box lock; top lever break-open; double triggers; hammerless
Magazine: None
Barrel: Double barrel, 26" to 32", any choke combination
Finish: Blued; checkered walnut straight or pistol grip stock & forearm
Estimated Value: $725.00 - $910.00

Bernardelli St. Uberto

Breda

Breda Autoloading

Breda Autoloading
Gauge: 12 regular or magnum; add 30% for magnum
Action: Semi-automatic; hammerless
Magazine: 4-shot tubular
Barrel: 25½" or 27½"
Finish: Blued; checkered walnut straight or pistol grip stock & forearm; available with ribbed barrel; engraving on grades 1, 2, & 3; engraved models worth more; estimated value for plain models
Estimated Value: $275.00 - $350.00

Browning BT-99 Trap

Browning BT-99 Trap
Gauge: 12
Action: Top lever break-open; automatic ejector; hammerless; single shot
Magazine: None
Barrel: 32" or 34" full, modified, or improved modified choke; or choke tubes; add 2% for choke tubes; high post ventilated rib
Finish: Blued; wide rib; checkered walnut pistol grip stock & forearm, some with Monte Carlo stock; recoil pad; some engraving; Pigeon Grade is satin gray steel with deep relief hand engraving
Estimated Value: $720.00 - $900.00

Browning Model BT-99 Plus
Gauge: 12
Action: Top lever, break-open; automatic ejector; hammerless; single shot
Magazine: None
Barrel: 32" or 34", choke tubes; high post, ventilated, tapered target rib with matted sight plane; front & center sight beads; ported barrel optional; add 1% for ported barrel
Finish: Blued; receiver engraved with rosette & scrolls; select walnut, checkered pistol grip stock & modified beavertail forearm; Monte Carlo style comb with recoil reducer system; adjustable for drop, cant, cast & length of pull; recoil pad
Estimated Value: $1,065.00 - $1,335.00

Browning Superposed

Browning Superposed Magnum Grade I
Same as the Superposed except: chambered for 3" magnum 12 gauge & recoil pad
Estimated Value: $1,200.00 - $3,600.00

Browning Superposed
Gauge: 12, 20, 28, or 410
Action: Non-selective trigger; double triggers; or selective trigger
Magazine: None
Barrel: Browning over & under double barrel; 26½", 28", 30", or 32"; any choke combination; ventilated or matted rib
Finish: Blued; hand-checkered European walnut pistol grip stock & forearm; fluted comb; recoil pad; engraving; made in many different grades; more inlays & engraving on higher grades
Estimated Value: $750.00 - $5,000.00

Browning

Browning Super Light
Similar to Superposed except: lightweight; 26½" barrel; straight grip stock; many grades
Estimated Value: $1,500.00 - $5,000.00

Browning Superposed Broadway Trap Grade I
Similar to Superposed except: wide ventilated rib; many grades
Estimated Value: $1,400.00 - $4,000.00

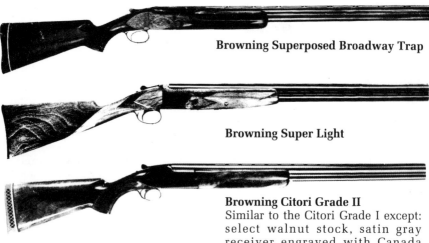

Browning Superposed Broadway Trap

Browning Super Light

Browning Citori Grade I

Browning Citori Grade II
Similar to the Citori Grade I except: select walnut stock, satin gray receiver engraved with Canada Goose & Ringneck Pheasant scenes; add 5% for 410 or 28 ga.
Estimated Value: $730.00 - $975.00

Browning Citori Grade I
Gauge: 12, 20, 28, or 410; regular & magnum; add 3% for 410 or 28 ga.
Action: Top lever break-open; hammerless; single selective trigger; automatic ejectors
Magazine: None
Barrel: Over & under double barrel; 26", 28, or 30" in a variety of choke combinations; or changable choke tubes; ventilated rib
Finish: Blued; checkered walnut stock & forearm; Hunting Model has pistol grip stock & beavertail forearm; Sporter has straight stock & lipped forearm; engraved receiver; high-polish finish on Hunting Model, oil finish on Sporter; Upland Special has straight stock; Lighting Model has rounded pistol grip; add 4% for Superlight or Upland Special
Estimated Value: $665.00 - $830.00

Browning Citori Grade III
Similar to the Grade II with grayed receiver, scroll engraving & mallards & ringnecks decoration; 20, 28, & 410 ga. have quail & grouse; add 10% for 28 or 410 ga.
Estimated Value: $985.00 - $1230.00

Browning Citori Grade V
Similar to the Citori Grade II with hand-checkered wood, hand-engraved receiver with Mallard Duck & Ringneck Pheasant scenes; add 5% for 410 or 28 gauge; add 3% for "Invector" choke tubes
Estimated Value: $1,100.00 - $1,475.00

Browning Citori Trap

Browning Citori Sideplate
Similar to the Citori Grade V in 20 gauge Sporter style only; 26" improved cylinder & modified or modified & full choke; sideplates & receiver are decorated with etched upland game scenes of doves, Ruffed Grouse, quail, & pointing dog
Estimated Value: $1,100.00 - $1,475.00

Browning Citori Skeet
Similar to the Citori Grade I except: 26" or 28" skeet choke barrels; high post target rib; add 43% for Grade II or Grade III decoration; add 100% for Grade VI
Estimated Value: $750.00 - $ 940.00

Browning Citori Trap
A trap version of the Citori Grade I in 12 gauge only; high post target rib; 30", 32", or 34" barrel; Monte Carlo stock; add 43% for Grade II or Grade III decoration; 100% for Grade VI
Estimated Value: $750.00 - $ 940.00

Browning Citori Grade VI
Similar to the Grade V Citori with grayed or blued receiver, deep relief engraving, gold plating & engraving of ringneck pheasants, mallard drakes & English Setter; add 10% for 28 gauge or 410
Estimated Value: $1415.00 - $1,770.00

Browning Citori Plus
Gauge: 12
Action: Top lever, break-open; hammerless; automatic ejectors
Magazine: None
Barrel: 30" or 32" over & under double barrel with high post, ventilated, tapered target rib; matted sight plane; choke tubes; front & center sight beads; ported barrel optional; add $50.00 for ported barrel
Finish: Blued; receiver engraving; select walnut checkered pistol grip stock & modified beavertail forearm; Monte Carlo style comb with recoil reduction system adjustable for drop, cant, cast & length of pull; recoil pad
Estimated Value: $1,135.00 - $1,415.00

Browning

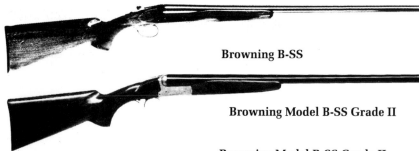

Browning B-SS

Browning Model B-SS Grade II

Browning B-SS
Gauge: 12 or 20
Action: Top lever break-open; hammerless; automatic ejectors; barrel selector; add 5% for barrel selector
Magazine: None
Barrel: Double barrel (side by side); 26", 28", or 30" in many choke combinations
Finish: Blued; checkered walnut pistol grip stock & forearm
Estimated Value: $435.00 - $580.00

Browning Model B-SS Grade II
Similar to the B-SS with engraved satin gray frame featuring a pheasant, ducks, and quail
Estimated Value: $650.00 - $850.00

Browning B-SS Sidelock
Similar to the Model B-SS with sidelock action, engraved gray receiver, double triggers, small tapered forearm & straight grip stock
Estimated Value: $915.00 - $1,280.00

Browning BPS

Browning BPS
Gauge: 10, 12, or 20; regular or magnum; add 32% for 10 gauge
Action: Slide action; concealed hammer; bottom ejection
Magazine: 4-shot; 3-shot in magnum
Barrel: 26", 28", 30" or 32" in many cokes; or choke tubes; ventilated rib
Finish: Blued; checkered walnut pistol grip stock & slide handle; trap Model has Monte Carlo stock; add 5% for Trap Model; Stalker Model has graphite-fiberglass composite stock with matte finish
Estimated Value: $265.00 - $330.00

Browning BPS Buck Special
Similar to the BPS with a 24" barrel for slugs; rifle sights; add 5% for strap & swivels
Estimated Value: $270.00 - $335.00

Browning BPS Youth and Ladies
Similar to the Model BPS in 20 gauge only with 22" barrel, compact stock & recoil pad
Estimated Value: $265.00 - $330.00

Browning BPS Upland Special

Browning BPS Upland Special
Similar to the BPS with a straight grip stock, 22" barrel and "Invector" choke tubes
Estimated Value: $265.00 - $330.00

Browning BPS Pigeon Grade Hunting
Same as the BPS except: 12 gauge only; select, high-grade stock and gold trim receiver; Invector chokes.
Estimated Value: $360.00 - $450.00

Browning BPS Deer Special
Similar to the BPS except: 12 gauge only; 20" barrel with 5" rifled slug choke tube; adjustable rear sight; scope mount base
Estimated Value: $300.00 - $375.00

Browning BPS Turkey Special
Similar to the BPS except: 12 gauge only; 20" barrel with newly designed extra full choke tube; receiver drilled and tapped for scope base
Estimated Value: $280.00 - $350.00

Browning Model 12

Browning Model 42, Grades I & V
Same as Browning Model 12, Grades I & V except: 410 gauge with 3" chamber; add 70% for Grade V
Estimated Value: $480.00 - $600.00

Browning Model 12, Grades I & V
Gauge: 20 or 28
Action: Slide action, repeating; concealed hammer
Magazine: 5-shot tubular; 2-shot with plug
Barrel: 26" modified, high ventilated rib
Finish: Blued; checkered walnut pistol grip stock & slide handle; Grade V has engraved receiver with gold plated scenes; add 60% for Grade V
Estimated Value: $440.00 - $550.00

Browning

Browning B.A.A.C. No. 1 Regular

Browning B.A.A.C. Two Shot

Browning B.A.A.C. No. 0 Messenger

Browning B.A.A.C. No. 1 Regular
Gauge: 12
Action: Semi-automatic, hammerless
Magazine: 4-shot
Barrel: 28"
Finish: Blued; walnut straight stock & grooved forearm
Estimated Value: $280.00 - $350.00

Browning B.A.A.C. No. 2 Trap
Trap Grade version of the No. 1 with some checkering
Estimated Value: $310.00 - $390.00

Browning B.A.A.C. Two Shot
Similar to the No. 1 except: 2-shot model
Estimated Value: $240.00 - $300.00

Browning B.A.A.C. No. 0 Messenger
A short, 20" barrel, version of the No. 1, made for bank guards, etc.
Estimated Value: $260.00 - $325.00

F.N. Browning Automatic
Similar to the B.A.A.C. No. 1 sold only overseas; some models have sling swivels
Estimated Value: $300.00 - $375.00

Browning Automatic 5 Standard Grade

Browning Automatic 5 Standard Grade
Gauge: 12, 16 , 20, or 410
Action: Semi-auto; hammerless; side ejection; recoiling barrel
Magazine: 4-shot, bottom load; 3-shot model also available
Barrel: 26"-32" full choke, modified or cylinder bore; plain, raised matted rib or ventilated rib; add 13% for ventilated rib
Finish: Blued; checkered walnut, pistol grip stock & forearm
Estimated Value: $490.00 - $600.00

Browning Automatic 5 Grades II, III, IV
Basically the same as the Standard Grade with engraving & improved quality on higher grades; add $50.00 for ventilated rib
Estimated Value: $500.00 - $2,000.00

Browning Automatic-5 Light 12

Browning Automatic-5 Light 20

Browning Auto-5 Trap
Basically the same as the Standard Grade except 12 gauge only; trap stock; 30" full choke barrel; ventilated rib; add 35% for Belgian-made.
Estimated Value: $440.00 - $550.00

Browning Auto-5 Light Skeet
Similar to the Light 12 & Light 20 with 26" or 28" skeet choke barrel; add 35% for Belgian-made
Estimated Value: $360.00 - $450.00

Browning Auto-5 Light 12
Basically the same as the Standard Grade except: 12 gauge only & lightweight; add 25% for Belgian-made; stalker model has graphite composite stock and non-glare finish
Estimated Value: $430.00 - $540.00

Browning Auto-5 Light 20
Basically the same as the Standard Grade except: 20 gauge only; lightweight 26" or 28" barrel; add 25% for Belgian-made
Estimated Value: $430.00 - $540.00

Browning

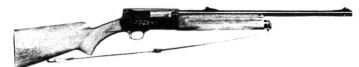

Browning Automatic-5 Light Buck Special

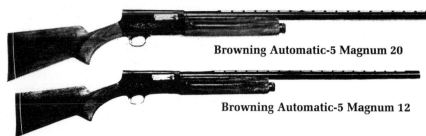

Browning Automatic-5 Magnum 20

Browning Automatic-5 Magnum 12

Browning Auto-5 Magnum 20
Similar to the Standard Model except 20 gauge magnum; 26" or 28" barrel; add 25% for Belgian-made
Estimated Value: $445.00 - $560.00

Browning Auto-5 Magnum 12
Similar to the Standard Model except: 12 gauge magnum with recoil pad; 32" full choke barrel; add 25% for Belgian-made; stalker model has graphite composite stock and non-glare finish
Estimated Value: $445.00 - $560.00

Browning Auto-5 Light Buck Special
Similar to the Standard Model 12 or 20 gauge except: special 24" barrel choked & bored for slug; add 4% for strap & swivels; add 25% for Belgian-made
Estimated Value: $435.00 - $545.00

Browning Auto-5 Buck Special Magnum
Same as the Buck Special except: 3" magnum in 12 & 20 gauge; add 4% for strap & swivels; add 25% for Belgian-made
Estimated Value: $450.00 - $560.00

Browning Automatic 5 Sweet Sixteen

Browning Auto-5 Sweet Sixteen
A lightweight 16 gauge version of the Standard Model Auto-5 with a gold plated trigger. Made from about 1936 to 1975 in Belgium; add 25% for Belgium-made
Estimated Value: $430.00 - $540.00

Browning Special (American-Made)
Similar to Grade I with a matted or
ventilated rib
Estimated Value: $310.00 - $390.00

Browning Grade I (American Made)

Browning Grade I (American-Made)
Similar to Browning Standard Grade
except: made by Remington from
1940 until about 1948. World War II
forced the closing of the plant in
Belgium
Estimated Value: $280.00 - $350.00

Browning Special Skeet (American-Made)
Same as the Grade I with a Cutts
Compensator
Estimated Value: $300.00 - $375.00

Browning Utility (American-Made)
Similar to Grade I with Poly-Choke
Estimated Value: $240.00 - $300.00

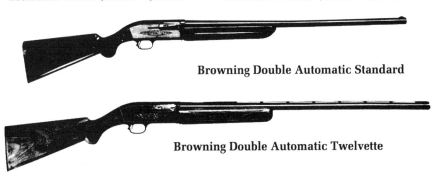

Browning Double Automatic Standard

Browning Double Automatic Twelvette

Browning Double Automatic Twelvette
Basically the same as the Standard
with lightweight aluminum receiver
Estimated Value: $360.00 - $450.00

Browning Double Automatic Twentyweight
A still lighter version of the Standard
in 20 ga. with 26½" barrel
Estimated Value: $365.00 - $460.00

Browning Double Automatic Standard
Gauge: 12
Action: Semi-automatic; short recoil,
side ejection; hammerless; 2-shot
Magazine: 1-shot
Barrel: 30" or 28" full choke; 28" or
26" modified choke; 28" or 26" skeet
choke; 26" cylinder bore or improved
cylinder; ventilated rib optional
Finish: Blued; checkered walnut
pistol grip stock & forearm; add 8%
for ventilated rib
Estimated Value: $320.00 - $400.00

Browning

Browning 2000

Browning Model B-2000 Trap

Browning Model B-2000 Trap & Skeet
Similar to the B-2000 with options of high-post ventilated rib & recoil pad on Trap Model.
Estimated Value: $300.00 - $400.00

Browning 2000 or B-2000
Similar to the Automatic 5 except: gas operated; in 12 or 20 gauge regular or magnum
Estimated Value: $280.00 - $375.00

Browning 2000 Buck Special
Similar to the 2000 except; 24" barrel; adjustable rifle sights; swivels
Estimated Value: $350.00 - $425.00

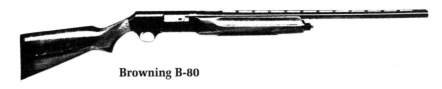

Browning B-80

Browning B-80 Buck Special
Similar to the B-80 except: 24" slug barrel; rifle sights; add $20.00 for strap & swivels
Estimated Value: $325.00 - $425.00

Browning B-80 Upland Special
Similar to the Model B-80 except: straight grip stock; 22" barrel
Estimated Value: $335.00 - $420.00

Browning B-80, B-80 Plus
Gauge: 12 or 20; regular or magnum
Action: Semi-automatic; gas operated
Magazine: 3-shot, 2-shot in magnum
Barrel: 26", 28", 30", or 32" in a variety of chokes or choke tubes; internally chrome plated; ventilated rib
Finish: Blued; checkered walnut semi-pistol grip stock & fluted, checkered forearm; alloy receiver on Superlight Model (B-80 Plus)
Estimated Value: $335.00 - $420.00

Browning Model A-500

Browning Model A-500
Gauge: 12; regular or magnum
Action: Short recoil operated semi-automatic
Magazine: 4-shot tubular; 3-shot in magnum; magazine cut-off allows chambering of shell independent of magazine
Barrel: 26", 28", or 30" with choke tubes; ventilated rib; 24" Buck Special barrel optional
Finish: Blued; checkered walnut pistol grip stock & forearm; recoil pad
Estimated Value: $330.00 - $415.00

Browning Model A-500G

Browning Model A-500R
Gauge: 12; regular or magnum
Action: Recoil operated, semi-automatic
Magazine: 4-shot; 3-shot in magnum
Barrel: 26", 28", or 30" with choke tubes; ventilated rib with matted sighting surface
Finish: Blued; red accents on receiver; select checkered walnut pistol grip stock & forearm; gold plated trigger
Estimated Value: $335.00 - $420.00

Browning Model A-500R Buck Special
Similar to the Model A-500R except: 24" slug barrel; adjustable rear sight
Estimated Value: $355.00 - $445.00

Browning Model A-500G
Gauge: 12; regular or magnum
Action: Gas operated, semi-automatic
Magazine: 4-shot; 3-shot in magnum shells
Barrel: 26", 28", or 30" barrel with choke tubes; ventilated rib with matted sighting surface
Finish: Blued; gold accents on receiver; select checkered walnut, pistol grip & forearm; recoil pad; gold trigger
Estimated Value: $385.00 - $480.00

Browning Model A-500G Buck Special
Similar to the Model A-500G except: 24" slug barrel & adjustable rear sight
Estimated Value: $400.00 - $500.00

Charles Daly

Charles Daly Single Barrel Trap

Charles Daly Commander 100
Gauge: 12, 16, 20, 28, or 410
Action: Box lock; top lever, break-open; hammerless; automatic ejectors
Magazine: None
Barrel: Over & under double barrel; 26", 28", or 30" improved cylinder & modified or modified & full chokes
Finish: Blued; checkered walnut straight or pistol grip stock & forearm; engraved
Estimated Value: $450.00 - $600.00

Charles Daly Commander 200
A fancier version of the Commander 100 with select wood, more engraving & a higher quality finish
Estimated Value: $620.00 - $775.00

Charles Daly Single Barrel Trap
Gauge: 12
Action: Box lock; top lever, break-open; hammerless; single shot
Magazine: None; single shot
Barrel: 32" or 34" full choke; ventilated rib
Finish: Blued; checkered walnut Monte Carlo pistol grip stock & beavertail forearm; recoil pad. This model should not be confused with the Single Barrel Trap Models made in the 1930's that are worth several times more
Estimated Value: $380.00 - $475.00

Charles Daly Hammerless Double
Gauge: 10, 12, 16, 20, 28 or 410
Action: Box lock; top lever, break-open; hammerless; automatic ejectors (except Superior)
Magazine: None
Barrel: Double barrel (side by side); 26", 28", 30", or 32"; many choke combinations
Finish: Blued; checkered walnut pistol grip stock & short tapered forearm; engraving; manufactured in many different grades; alike except for quality of finish & amount of engraving
Estimated Value: $1,200.00 - $4,500.00

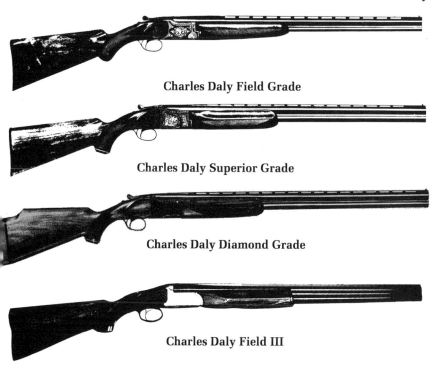

Charles Daly Field Grade

Charles Daly Superior Grade

Charles Daly Diamond Grade

Charles Daly Field III

Charles Daly Field Grade
Gauge: 12, 20, 28, or 410 regular; 12 or 20 magnum
Action: Box lock; top lever, break-open; hammerless; single trigger
Magazine: None
Barrel: Over & under double barrel; 26", 28", or 30"; many choke combinations; ventilated rib
Finish: Blued; engraved; checkered walnut pistol grip stock & forearm; 12 gauge magnum has recoil pad
Estimated Value: $410.00 - $550.00

Charles Daly Superior Grade
Similar to the Field Grade except: not chambered for magnum
Estimated Value: $430.00 - $575.00

Charles Daly Diamond Grade
Similar to the Superior with select wood & fancier engraving
Estimated Value: $560.00 - $700.00

Charles Daly Field III
Similar to the Field Grade with some minor changes; double trigger
Estimated Value: $265.00 - $335.00

Charles Daly Superior II
Similar to the Field III but higher quality
Estimated Value: $420.00 - $525.00

Charles Daly

Charles Daly Venture Grade

Charles Daly Auto

Charles Daly Auto Superior

Charles Daly Venture Grade
Gauge: 12 or 20
Action: Box lock; top lever, break-open; hammerless; automatic ejectors
Magazine: None
Barrel: Over & under double barrel; 26", 28", or 30", various chokes; ventilated rib
Finish: Blued; checkered walnut pistol grip stock & forearm; add $25.00 for Skeet Model; add $35.00 for Trap Model
Estimated Value: $340.00 - $425.00

Charles Daly Auto Field
Gauge: 12 regular or magnum
Action: Semi-automatic, recoil operated
Magazine: 5-shot tubular
Barrel: 26" improved cylinder or skeet, 28" modified or full, 30" full, choke; ventilated rib
Finish: Blued; checkered walnut pistol grip stock & forearm
Estimated Value: $240.00 - $300.00

Charles Daly Auto Superior
Similar to the Auto Field but higher quality
Estimated Value: $260.00 - $325.00

Colt

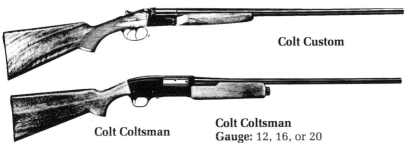

Colt Custom

Colt Coltsman

Colt Custom
Gauge: 12 or 16
Action: Box lock; top lever, break-open; hammerless; double trigger; automatic ejectors
Magazine: None
Barrel: Double barrel (side by side); 26" improved & modified, 28" modified & full or 30" full chokes
Finish: Blued; checkered walnut pistol grip stock & tapered forearm
Estimated Value: $300.00 - $390.00

Colt Coltsman
Gauge: 12, 16, or 20
Action: Side action
Magazine: 4-shot
Barrel: 26" improved, 28" modified, 30" full choke
Finish: Blued; plain walnut pistol grip stock & slide handle
Estimated Value: $180.00 - $225.00

Colt Coltsman Custom
A fancier version of the Coltsman with checkering & ventilated rib
Estimated Value: $210.00 - $260.00

Colt Ultra Light

Colt Ultra Light Custom
Same as the Ultra Light except: select wood, engraving & ventilated rib
Estimated Value: $250.00 - $320.00

Colt Ultra Light
Gauge: 12 or 20
Action: Semi-automatic
Magazine: 4-shot
Barrel: Chrome lined; 26" improved or modified; 28" modified or full; 30" or 32" full choke; rib optional; add $15.00 for solid rib; add $25.00 for ventilated rib
Finish: Blued; checkered walnut pistol grip stock & forearm; alloy receiver
Estimated Value: $220.00 - $275.00

Colt Magnum Auto
Same as the Ultra Light except: magnum gauges & of heavier weight; add $15.00 for solid rib; add $25.00 for ventilated rib
Estimated Value: $240.00 - $300.00

Colt Magnum Auto Custom
Same as Magnum Auto except: select wood, engraving & ventilated rib
Estimated Value: $260.00 - $325.00

Darne

Darne Sliding Breech Double

Darne Sliding Breech Double
Gauge: 12, 16, 20, or 28
Action: Sliding breech; selective ejectors; double trigger
Magazine: None
Barrel: Double barrel (side by side); 25½" or 27½" modified & improved cylinder choke; raised rib
Finish: Blued; checkered walnut straight or pistol grip stock & forearm
Estimated Value: $600.00 - $800.00

Darne Deluxe
Same as the Sliding Breech Double with engraving & 28" modified & full choke barrels
Estimated Value: $825.00 - $1,100.00

Darne Supreme
Same as the Darne Deluxe except: 20 or 28 gauge; 25½" barrels; elaborate engraving & swivels
Estimated Value: $1,200.00 - $1,500.00

Darne Deluxe

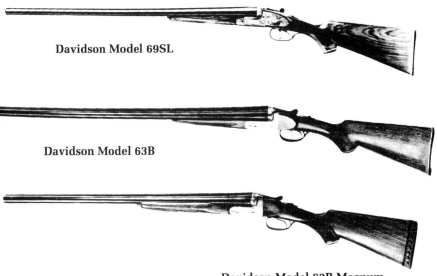

Davidson Model 69SL

Davidson Model 63B

Davidson Model 63B Magnum

Davidson Model 73 Stagecoach
Gauge: 12 or 20 magnum
Action: Box lock; top lever break-open; exposed hammers
Magazine: None
Barrel: Double barrel (side by side); 20" improved cylinder & modified or modified & full chokes; matted rib
Finish: Blued; checkered walnut pistol grip stock & forearm; sights; engraved receiver
Estimated Value: $190.00 - $240.00

Davidson Model 69 SL
Gauge: 12 or 20
Action: Side lock, hammerless
Magazine: None
Barrel: Double barrel (side by side); 26", 28", or 30"; variety of chokes
Finish: Blued or nickel; checkered walnut pistol grip stock & forearm; gold plated trigger; engraved
Estimated Value: $240.00 - $300.00

Davidson Model 63B
Gauge: 12, 16, 20, 28, or 410
Action: Box lock; top lever break-open; double triggers
Magazine: None
Barrel: Double barrel (side by side); 25" (410), 26", 28", or 30" in other gauges; any choke combination
Finish: Blued or nickel; checkered walnut pistol grip stock & forearm; some engraving
Estimated Value: $220.00 - $275.00

Davidson Model 63B Magnum
Same as Model 63B except: 10, 12, or 20 gauge magnum; available with 32" barrel in 10 gauge
Estimated Value: $235.00 - $295.00

Fox

Fox Trap (Single Barrel)
Gauge: 12
Action: Box lock; top lever break-open; hammerless; automatic ejector; single shot
Magazine: None; single shot
Barrel: 30" or 32" trap bore; ventilated rib
Finish: Blued; checkered walnut half or full pistol grip stock & forearm; decorated receiver; grades differ in quality of craftsmanship & decoration; some have Monte Carlo stock; ME Grade was made to order with inlaid gold & finest walnut wood
Estimated Value:
  GRADES
  JE: $1,200.00 - $1,600.00
  KE: $1,400.00 - $2,000.00
  LE: $1,400.00 - $2,500.00
  ME: $4,000.00 - $5,500.00

Fox Trap (Single Barrel)

Fox Sterlingworth
Gauge: 12, 16, or 20
Action: Box lock; top lever break-open; hammerless; double trigger or selective single trigger; some with automatic ejectors; add 10% for selective trigger; add 12% for automatic ejectors
Magazine: None
Barrel: Double barrel (side by side); 26", 28", or 30"; full & full, modified & full, cylinder & modified chokes
Finish: Blued; checkered walnut pistol grip stock & forearm
Estimated Value: $490.00 - $600.00

Fox Sterlingworth Skeet
Same as the Sterlingworth except: skeet bore; 26" or 28" barrels; straight grip stock; add 12% for automatic ejectors
Estimated Value: $560.00 - $690.00

Fox Sterlingworth

Fox Skeeter
Similar to Sterlingworth except: 28" skeet bored barrels; ventilated rib; ivory bead; recoil pad; 12 or 20 gauge; automatic ejectors
Estimated Value: $750.00 - $1,000.00

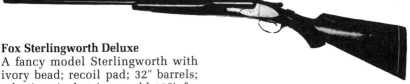

Fox Sterlingworth Deluxe
A fancy model Sterlingworth with ivory bead; recoil pad; 32" barrels; selective single trigger; add 10% for automatic ejectors
Estimated Value: $575.00 - $700.00

Fox Sterlingworth Deluxe

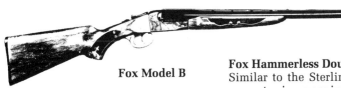

Fox Model B

Fox Model B, BE
Gauge: 12, 16, 20, or 410
Action: Box lock; top lever break-open; hammerless; double triggers; Model BE has automatic ejectors; add $60.00 for model BE
Magazine: None
Barrel: Double barrel (side by side); 24", 26", 28", or 30'; in almost any choke combination; ventilated rib
Finish: Blued; checkered walnut pistol grip stock & forearm
Estimated Value: $230.00 - $290.00

Fox Model B Lightweight
Same as the Model B except: 24" cylinder bore & modified choke barrels in 12 & 20 gauge
Estimated Value: $210.00 - $265.00

Fox Hammerless Doubles
Similar to the Sterlingworth models except: in varying degrees of increased quality. All have automatic ejectors except Grade A; add $60.00 for selective single trigger; $125.00 for ventilated rib
Estimated Value:
Grade
A: $650.00 - $850.00
AE: $950.00 - $1,200.00
BE: $1,200.00 - $1,600.00
CE: $1,300.00 - $1,700.00
DE: $2,275.00 - $3,000.00

Fox Super Fox
Gauge: 12
Action: Box lock; top lever break-open; hammerless; double trigger; automatic ejectors
Magazine: None
Barrel: Double barrel (side by side); 30" or 32" full choke
Finish: Blued; checkered walnut pistol grip stock & forearm
Estimated Value: $520.00 - $650.00

Fox

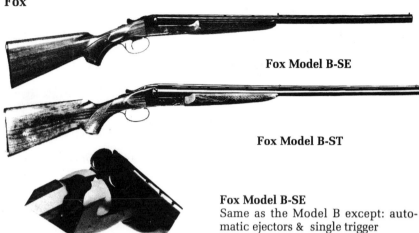

Fox Model B-SE

Fox Model B-ST

Fox Model BDL

Fox Model B-DL & B-DE
Similar to the B-ST except: chrome
receiver & beavertail forearm
Estimated Value: $275.00 - $350.00

Fox Model B-SE
Same as the Model B except: auto-
matic ejectors & single trigger
Estimated Value: $260.00 - $350.00

Fox Model B-ST
Same as Model B except: gold
plated non-selective single trigger
Estimated Value: $250.00 - $325.00

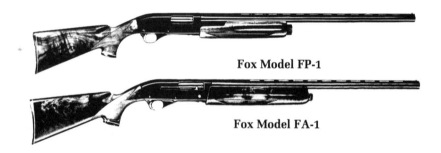

Fox Model FP-1

Fox Model FA-1

Fox Model FP-1
Gauge: 12 (2¾" or 3")
Action: Slide action, hammerless
Magazine: 4-shot tubular; 3-shot
with 3" shells
Barrel: 28" modified; 30" full choke;
ventilated rib
Finish: Blued; checkered walnut
pistol grip stock & slide handle;
rosewood cap with inlay
Estimated Value: $220.00 - $275.00

Fox Model FA-1
Gauge: 12 (2¾")
Action: Semi-automatic; gas operated
Magazine: 3-shot tubular
Barrel: 28" modified; 30" full choke;
ventilated rib
Finish: Blued; checkered walnut
pistol grip stock & forearm; rosewood
cap with inlay
Estimated Value: $230.00 - $290.00

Franchi

Franchi Airone

Franchi Airone
Gauge: 12
Action: Box lock; top lever, break-open; hammerless; automatic ejectors
Magazine: None
Barrel: Double barrel (side by side); several lengths & choke combinations
Finish: Blued; checkered walnut straight grip stock & short tapered forearm; engraving
Estimated Value: $700.00 - $875.00

Franchi Astore
Gauge: 12
Action: Box lock; top lever, break-open; hammerless; double triggers
Magazine: None
Barrel: Double barrel (side by side); several lengths & choke combinations available
Finish: Blued; checkered walnut straight grip stock & short tapered forearm
Estimated Value: $680.00 - $850.00

Franchi Astore S
Same as the Astore except: higher quality wood & engraving
Estimated Value: $1,000.00 - $1,250.00

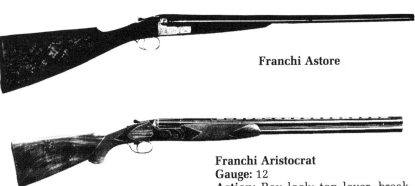

Franchi Astore

Franchi Aristocrat

Franchi Aristocrat
Gauge: 12
Action: Box lock; top lever, break-open; hammerless; automatic ejectors; single trigger
Magazine: None
Barrel: Over & under double barrel; 24" cylinder bore & improved cylinder; 26" improved cylinder & modified, 28" or 30" modified & full chokes; ventilated rib
Finish: Blued; checkered walnut pistol grip stock & forearm; engraving
Estimated Value: $470.00 - $590.00

Franchi Aristocrat Skeet
Same as the Aristocrat Trap except: 26" skeet barrels
Estimated Value: $540.00 - $675.00

Franchi

Franchi Aristocrat Trap

Franchi Aristocrat Silver King
Similar to the Aristocrat except: higher quality finish; select wood; engraving
Estimated Value: $580.00 - $725.00

Franchi Aristocrat Trap
Similar to the Aristocrat except: Monte Carlo stock; chrome lined barrels; case hardened receiver; 30" barrels
Estimated Value: $520.00 - $650.00

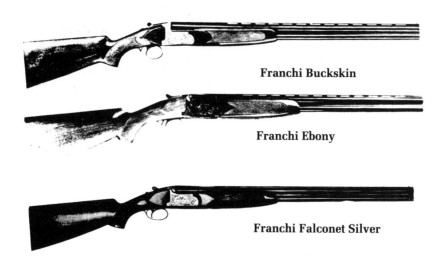

Franchi Buckskin

Franchi Ebony

Franchi Falconet Silver

Franchi Falconet Buckskin & Ebony
Gauge: 12 or 20
Action: Box lock; top lever, break-open; hammerless
Magazine: None
Barrel: Over & under double barrel; chrome lined; 24", 26", 28", or 30" barrels in several choke combinations; ventilated rib
Finish: Blued; colored frame with engraving; epoxy finished checkered walnut pistol grip stock & forearm; Buckskin & Ebony differ only in color of receiver & engraving
Estimated Value: $470.00 - $590.00

Franchi Falconet Silver
Same as the Falconet Buckskin & Ebony except: 12 gauge only; pickled silver receiver
Estimated Value: $500.00 - $625.00

Franchi Falconet Super
Similar to the Falconet Silver except: slightly different forearm; 12 gauge only; 27" or 28" barrels
Estimated Value: $520.00 - $650.00

Franchi Peregrine 400

Franchi Peregrine 451
Similar to the 400 except: lightweight alloy receiver
Estimated Value: $440.00 - $550.00

Franchi Peregrine 400
Gauge: 12 or 20
Action: Box lock; top lever, break-open; hammerless
Magazine: None
Barrel: Over & under double barrel; 26½", 28" in various chokes; chrome lined; ventilated rib
Finish: Blued; checkered walnut pistol grip stock & forearm
Estimated Value: $460.00 - $585.00

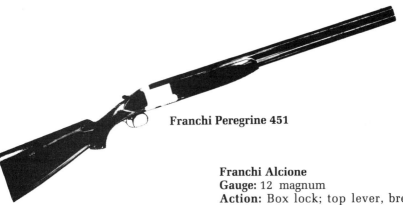

Franchi Peregrine 451

Franchi Diamond
Gauge: 12
Action: Box lock; top lever, break-open; hammerless; single selective trigger; automatic extractors
Magazine: None
Barrel: Over & under double barrel; 28" modified & full choke; ventilated rib
Finish: Blued; checkered walnut pistol grip stock & forearm; silver plated receiver
Estimated Value: $540.00 - $675.00

Franchi Alcione
Gauge: 12 magnum
Action: Box lock; top lever, break-open; hammerless; single selective trigger; automatic split selective ejectors
Magazine: None
Barrel: Over & under double barrel; 26" improved cylinder & modified; 28" modified & full choke; ventilated rib
Finish: Blued; coin-finished steel receiver with scroll engraving; checkered walnut pistol grip stock & forearm; recoil pad
Estimated Value: $440.00 - $550.00

Franchi

Franchi Standard Model

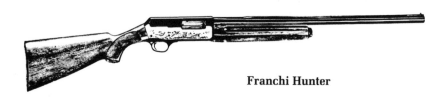

Franchi Hunter

Franchi Standard Model, 48AL
Gauge: 12, 20, or 28
Action: Semi-automatic; recoil operated
Magazine: 5-shot tubular
Barrel: 24" or 26" improved cylinder, modified or skeet; 28" modified or full chokes; chrome lined; ventilated rib on some
Finish: Blued; checkered walnut pistol grip stock with fluted forearm
Estimated Value: $280.00 - $350.00

Franchi Hunter, 48AL
Similar to the Standard Model except: 12 or 20 gauge; higher quality wood; engraving; ventilated rib
Estimated Value: $300.00 - $390.00

Franchi Hunter Magnum
Same as the Hunter except: recoil pad; chambered for 12 or 20 ga. mag.
Estimated Value: $320.00 - $400.00

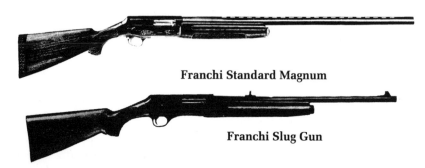

Franchi Standard Magnum

Franchi Slug Gun

Franchi Standard Magnum, 48AL
Similar to the Standard model, 48AL except: recoil pad; chambered for magnum shells; 12 or 20 gauge
Estimated Value: $300.00 - $375.00

Franchi Slug Gun, 48AL
Similar to the Standard Model, 48AL except: 22" cylinder bore barrel; sights; swivels; alloy receiver 12 or 20 gauge
Estimated Value: $280.00 - $350.00

Pocket Guide to Shotguns

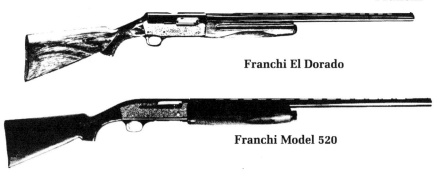

Franchi El Dorado

Franchi Model 520

Franchi Prestige

Franchi Eldorado
Similar to the Standard Model, AL
except: heavy engraving; select wood;
gold plated trigger; ventilated rib
Estimated Value: $380.00 - $475.00

Franchi Model 500
Similar to the Standard model, 48AL
except: gas operated; 12 gauge only;
made for fast takedown
Estimated Value: $280.00 - $350.00

Franchi Model 520
Similar to the Model 500 with
deluxe features
Estimated Value: $320.00 - $300.00

Franchi Model 530 Trap
Similar to the Model 520 except:
Monte Carlo stock; high ventilated
rib; three interchangeable choke tubes
Estimated Value: $440.00 - $550.00

Franchi Elite
Similar to the Prestige with higher
quality finish. Receiver has acid-
etched wildlife scenes
Estimated Value: $325.00 - $410.00

Franchi Prestige, PG 85MA
Gauge: 12 regular or magnum
Action: Gas operated, semi-automatic
Magazine: 5-shot tubular (2¾"
shells)
Barrel: 24" slug; 26" improved
cylinder or modified, 28" modified
or full, 30" full; chrome lined;
ventilated rib
Finish: Blued; checkered walnut
pistol grip stock & fluted forearm;
sights on slug barrel
Estimated Value: $300.00 - $375.00

Greifelt

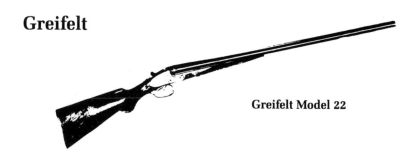

Greifelt Model 22

Greifelt Model 22
Gauge: 12 or 16
Action: Box lock; top lever, break-open; hammerless; double trigger
Magazine: None
Barrel: Double barrel (side by side); 28" or 30" modified or full chokes
Finish: Blued; checkered walnut straight or pistol grip stock & forearm
Estimated Value: 1,200.00 - $1,500.00

Greifelt Model 22E
Same as Model 22 with automatic ejector
Estimated Value: $1,260.00 - $1,575.00

Greifelt Model 103
Gauge: 12 or 16
Action: Box lock; top lever, break-open; hammerless; double triggers
Magazine: None
Barrel: Double barrel (side by side); 28" or 30" modified & full chokes
Finish: Blued; checkered walnut straight or pistol grip stock & forearm
Estimated Value: $1,100.00 - $1,375.00

Greifelt Model 103E
Same as the Model 103 with automatic ejectors
Estimated Value: $1,180.00 - $1,475.00

Harrington & Richardson

Harrington & Richardson No. 3

H & R No. 3
Gauge: 12, 16, 20, or 410
Action: Box lock; top lever, break-open; hammerless; single shot; automatic extractor
Magazine: None
Barrel: 26", 28", 30", or 32" full choke
Finish: Blued; walnut semi-pistol grip stock & tapered forearm
Estimated Value: $75.00 - $95.00

H & R No. 5
Gauge: 20, 28, or 410
Action: Box lock; top lever, break-open; exposed hammer; single shot; automatic extractor
Magazine: None
Barrel: 26" or 28" full choke
Finish: Blued; walnut semi-pistol grip stock & tapered forearm
Estimated Value: $80.00 - $100.00

Harrington & Richardson No. 5

H & R No. 6
Similar to the No. 5 except: 10, 12, 16, or 20 gauge; heavier design; barrel lengths of 28", 30", 32", 34", or 36"
Estimated Value: $85.00 - $110.00

Harrington & Richardson No. 6

H & R No. 8
Similar to the No. 6 with different style forearm & in 12, 16, 20, 24, 28 & 410 gauges
Estimated Value: $65.00 - $80.00

Harrington & Richardson No. 8

H & R No. 7 or No. 9
Similar to the No. 8 with smaller forearm & more rounded pistol grip; not available in 24 gauge
Estimated Value: $65.00 - $85.00

Harrington & Richardson No. 7

Harrington & Richardson Topper No. 48

H & R Topper No. 48
Similar to the No. 8. Made from the mid 1940's to the late 1950's
Estimated Value: $70.00 - $90.00

Harrington & Richardson

H & R Topper No. 488 Deluxe
Similar to the No. 48 except: chrome receiver; recoil pad; black lacquered stock & forearm
Estimated Value: $75.00 - $95.00

H & R Topper Jr. 480
Youth version of the No. 48; 410 gauge; 26" barrel; smaller stock
Estimated Value: $60.00 - $75.00

H & R Topper Jr. 580
Similar to the Topper Jr. 480 except: color finish similar to 188 Deluxe
Estimated Value: $65.00 - $80.00

H & R Folding Model
Gauge: 28 or 410 with light frame; 12, 16, 20, 28, or 410 with heavy frame
Action: Box lock; top lever, break-open; exposed hammer; single shot
Magazine: None
Barrel: 22" in light frame; 26" in heavy frame; full choke
Finish: Blued; walnut semi-pistol grip stock & tapered forearm; sight
Estimated Value: $95.00 - $120.00

Harrington & Richardson Folding Model

Harrington & Richardson Topper 158

H & R Topper 188 Deluxe
Similar to the No. 148 with black, red, blue, green, pink, yellow or purple lacquered finish; chrome plated frame; 410 gauge only
Estimated Value: $65.00 - $80.00

H & R Topper 158 or 058
Gauge: 12, 16, 20, 28, or 410
Action: Box lock; side lever, break-open; exposed hammer; single shot; Also available in 058 combination with 22" rifle barrel in 22 Hornet or 30-30 Win.; add 20% for extra barrel
Magazine: None
Barrel: 28", 30", 32", 34", or 36"; variety of chokes
Finish: Blued; plain wood, straight or semi-pistol grip stock & tapered forearm
Estimated Value: $75.00 - $95.00

H & R No. 148
Gauge: 12, 16, 20, or 410
Action: Box lock; top lever, break-open; hammerless; single shot; automatic extractor
Magazine: None
Barrel: 28", 30", 32", 34", or 36"; full choke
Finish: Blued; walnut semi-pistol grip stock & forearm; recoil pad
Estimated Value: $70.00 - $85.00

Harrington & Richardson

Harrington & Richardson Model 099 Deluxe

Harrington & Richardson Topper 198

Harrington & Richardson Topper 490

Harrington & Richardson Topper Buck 162

H & R Model 258 Handy Gun
Similar to the Model 058 combination shotgun/rifle with nickel finish; 22" barrel; 20 gauge with 22 Hornet, 30-30, 44 magnum, 357 magnum or 357 Maximum rifle barrel
Estimated Value: $140.00 - $175.00

H & R Model 099 Deluxe
Similar to the Model 158 with electro-less matte nickel finish
Estimated Value: $65.00 - $85.00

H & R Topper 198 or 098
Similar to the Model 158 or 058 except: 20 or 410 gauge only; black lacquered stock & forearm; nickel plated receiver
Estimated Value: $ 80.00 - $100.00

H & R Topper 490 &
490 Greenwing
A youth version of the Model 158 & 058 with 26" barrel; shorter stock; 20, 28, or 410 gauges only; Greenwing has higher quality finish
Estimated Value: $65.00 - $85.00

H& R Topper 590
Similar to the 490 with chrome plated receiver & color lacquered stock & forearm
Estimated Value: $70.00 - $90.00

H & R Topper Buck 162
Similar to the Model 158 & 058 except: 24" cylinder bore barrel for slugs; equipped with sights
Estimated Value: $ 80.00 - $100.00

Harrington & Richardson

Harrington & Richardson Golden Squire 159

Harrington & Richardson Model 176

H & R Model 176
Gauge: 10, 12, 16, or 20 regular or magnum
Action: Box lock; top lever, break-open; exposed hammer; single shot
Magazine: None
Barrel: 32" or 36" full choke in 10 or 12 gauge; 32" full choke in 16 or 20 gauge
Finish: Blued; case hardened receiver; plain hardwood Monte Carlo pistol grip stock & forearm; recoil pad
Estimated Value: $80.00 - $100.00

H & R Golden Squire 159
Gauge: 12 or 20
Action: Box lock; top lever, break-open; exposed hammer; single shot; automatic ejector
Magazine: None
Barrel: 28" or 30"; full choke
Finish: Blued; wood, straight grip stock & lipped forearm; recoil pad
Estimated Value: $80.00 - $100.00

H & R Golden Squire Jr. 459
Similar to the 159 except: 26" barrel & shorter stock
Estimated Value: $75.00 - $95.00

H & R Model 176 Slug
Similar to the Model 176 except: 28" cylinder bore slug barrel; rifle sights; swivels
Estimated Value: $85.00 - $115.00

Harrington & Richardson Model 088

H & R Model 088
Gauge: 12, 16, 20, or 410 regular or magnum
Action: Box lock; top lever, break-open; exposed hammer; single shot
Magazine: None
Barrel: 28" modified or full in 12 gauge; 28" modified in 16 gauge; 26" modified or full in 20 gauge; 25" full in 410
Finish: Blued; case hardened receiver; plain hardwood semi-pistol grip stock & forearm
Estimated Value: $70.00 - $90.00

H & R Model 088 Jr.
Similar to the Model 088 with a scaled-down stock & forearm; 25" barrel in 20 or 410 gauge
Estimated Value: $75.00 - $95.00

Pocket Guide to Shotguns

Harrington & Richardson 404

H & R Model 404C
Same as model 404 except: Monte Carlo stock
Estimated Value: $150.00 - $200.00

H & R Model 404
Gauge: 12, 20, or 410
Action: Box lock; side lever, break-open
Magazine: None
Barrel: Double barrel (side by side); 26" or 28"; variety of choke combinations
Finish: Blued; checkered wood semi-pistol grip stock & forearm
Estimated Value: $155.00 - $195.00

Harrington & Richardson Model 1212

H & R Gamester 348
Gauge: 12 or 16
Action: Bolt action; repeating
Magazine: 2-shot
Barrel: 28" full choke
Finish: Blued; plain wood, semi-pistol grip stock & forearm
Estimated Value: $70.00 - $90.00

H & R Model 1212
Gauge: 12
Action: Box lock; top lever, break-open; single selective trigger
Magazine: None
Barrel: Over & under double barrel; 28" improved modified over improved cylinder; ventilated rib
Finish: Blued; decorated frame; checkered walnut pistol grip stock & forearm
Estimated Value: $270.00 - $335.00

H & R Gamester 349 Deluxe
Same as Gamester 348 except: adjustable choke; 26" barrel; recoil pad
Estimated Value: $ 80.00 - $100.00

H & R Model 1212 Waterfowl
Similar to the Model 1212 in 12 gauge magnum; 30" full choke over modified barrel; ventilated recoil pad
Estimated Value: $290.00 - $350.00

Harrington & Richardson

Harrington & Richardson Model 400

H & R Huntsman 351
Gauge: 12 or 16
Action: Bolt action; repeating
Magazine: 2-shot tubular
Barrel: 26"; adjustable choke
Finish: Blued; plain Monte Carlo semi-pistol grip stock & forearm; recoil pad
Estimated Value: $75.00 - $95.00

H & R Model 400
Gauge: 12, 16, or 20
Action: Slide action; hammerless; repeating
Magazine: 5-shot tubular
Barrel: 28" full choke
Finish: Blued; semi-pistol grip stock & grooved slide handle
Estimated Value: $130.00 - $160.00

Harrington & Richardson Model 402

H & R Model 401
Same as the 400 except: adjustable choke
Estimated Value: $130.00 - $165.00

H & R Model 402
Similar to the model 400 except: 410 gauge only
Estimated Value: $135.00 - $170.00

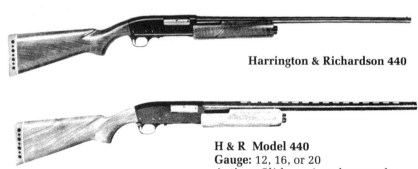

Harrington & Richardson 440

Harrington & Richardson 442

H & R Model 440
Gauge: 12, 16, or 20
Action: Slide action; hammerless; repeating
Magazine: 4-shot clip
Barrel: 24", 26", or 28"; variety of chokes
Finish: Blued; walnut semi-pistol grip stock & forearm; recoil pad
Estimated Value: $130.00 - $165.00

H & R Model 442
Similar to the model 440 except: ventilated rib & checkering
Estimated Value: $145.00 - $180.00

Harrington & Richardson/ High Standard

Harrington & Richardson 403

H & R Model 403
Gauge: 410
Action: Semi-automatic
Magazine: 4-shot tubular
Barrel: 26" full choke
Finish: Blued; wood semi-pistol grip stock & fluted forearm
Estimated Value: $175.00 - $225.00

High Standard

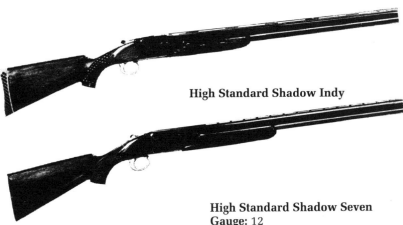

High Standard Shadow Indy

High Standard Shadow Seven

High Standard Shadow Seven
Gauge: 12
Action: Box lock; top lever, break-open; hammerless; single selective trigger; automatic ejectors
Magazine: None
Barrel: Over & under double barrel; 27½" or 29½"; variety of chokes; ventilated rib
Finish: Blued; checkered walnut pistol grip stock & forearm; gold plated trigger
Estimated Value: $440.00 - $550.00

High Standard Shadow Indy
Similar to Shadow Seven except: higher quality finish; chrome lined barrels; engraving
Estimated Value: $540.00 - $675.00

High Standard

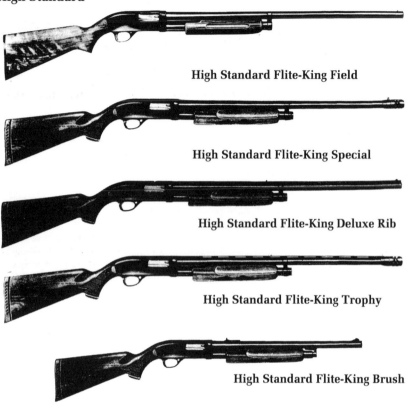

High Standard Flite-King Field

High Standard Flite-King Special

High Standard Flite-King Deluxe Rib

High Standard Flite-King Trophy

High Standard Flite-King Brush

High Standard Flite-King Field
Gauge: 12, 16, 20, or 410
Action: Slide action; hammerless; repeating
Magazine: 5-shot tubular; 4-shot tubular in 20 gauge
Barrel: 26" improved cylinder; 28" modified; 30" full choke
Finish: Blued; plain walnut semi-pistol grip stock & grooved slide handle
Estimated Value: $130.00 - $165.00

High Standard Flite-King Special
Similar to Flite-King Field except: adjustable choke & 27" barrel; no 410 gauge
Estimated Value: $135.00 - $170.00

High Standard Flite-King Deluxe Rib
Similar to the Flite-King Field except: ventilated rib & checkered wood
Estimated Value: $145.00 - $180.00

High Standard Flite-King Trophy
Similar to the Flight-King Deluxe Rib except: adjustable choke & 27" barrel; no 410 gauge
Estimated Value: $150.00 - $190.00

High Standard Flite-King Brush
Similar to Flite-King Field except: 18" or 20" cylinder bore barrel; rifle sights; 12 gauge only
Estimated Value: $140.00 - $185.00

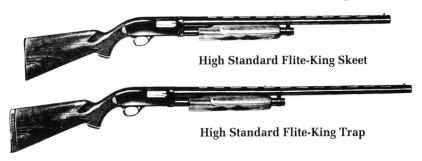

High Standard Flite-King Skeet

High Standard Flite-King Trap

High Standard Flite-King Skeet
Similar to the Flight-King Deluxe Rib except: skeet choke; 26" ventilated rib barrel; no 16 gauge
Estimated Value: $155.00 - $195.00

High Standard Flite-King Trap
Similar to the Flight-King Deluxe Rib except: 30" full choke barrel; trap stock; 26" barrel in 410 gauge
Estimated Value: $155.00 - $195.00

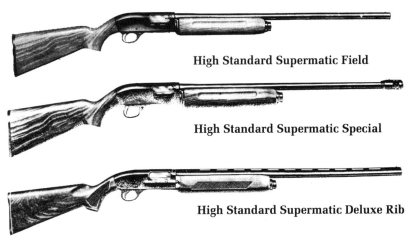

High Standard Supermatic Field

High Standard Supermatic Special

High Standard Supermatic Deluxe Rib

High Standard Supermatic Field
Gauge: 12 or 20; 20 magnum
Action: Semi-automatic, gas operated; hammerless
Magazine: 4-shot tubular; 3-shot tubular in 20 magnum
Barrel: 26", 28", or 30"; many chokes
Finish: Blued; plain walnut semi-pistol grip stock & fluted forearm
Estimated Value: $175.00 - $220.00

High Standard Supermatic Special
Similar to the Supermatic Field except: adjustable choke & 27" barrel
Estimated Value: $185.00 - $230.00

High Standard Supermatic Deluxe Rib
Similar to Supermatic Field except: 28" modified or full choke barrel, (30" in 12 gauge); checkered wood & ventilated rib
Estimated Value: $190.00 - $235.00

High Standard

High Standard Supermatic Trophy

High Standard Supermatic Duck

High Standard Supermatic Trap

High Standard Shadow Automatic

High Standard Supermatic Trophy
Similar to the Supermatic Field with a 27" barrel; adjustable choke; ventilated rib; checkering
Estimated Value: $200.00 - $250.00

High Standard Supermatic Skeet
Similar to Supermatic Field Model except: 26" ventilated rib barrel; skeet choke; checkered wood
Estimated Value: $210.00 - $260.00

High Standard Supermatic Duck
Similar to the Supermatic Field except: 12 gauge magnum with a 30" full choke barrel & recoil pad
Estimated Value: $190.00 - $240.00

High Standard Supermatic Duck Rib
Similar to the Supermatic Duck except: checkered wood & ventilated rib
Estimated Value: $200.00 - $250.00

High Standard Supermatic Trap
Similar to the Supermatic Field in 12 gauge only; 30" full choke; ventilated rib; checkered trap stock & forearm; recoil pad
Estimated Value: $200.00 - $245.00

High Standard Shadow Automatic
Gauge: 12 or 20; regular or magnum
Action: Semi-automatic; gas operated; hammerless
Magazine: 4-shot tubular
Barrel: 26", 28", or 30"; variety of chokes; ventilated rib
Finish: Blued; walnut pistol grip stock & forearm
Estimated Value: $210.00 - $260.00

Hunter

Hunter Fulton

Hunter Fulton
Gauge: 12, 16, or 20
Action: Box lock; top lever, break-open; hammerless; double or single trigger; add $50.00 for single trigger
Magazine: None
Barrel: Double barrel (side by side); 26", 28", 30", or 32"; various choke combinations
Finish: Blued; checkered walnut pistol grip stock & forearm
Estimated Value: $400.00 - $500.00

Hunter Special
Similar to Hunter Fulton except: higher quality; add $50.00 for single trigger
Estimated Value: $490.00 - $650.00

Ithaca

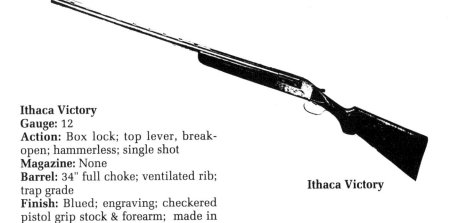

Ithaca Victory
Gauge: 12
Action: Box lock; top lever, break-open; hammerless; single shot
Magazine: None
Barrel: 34" full choke; ventilated rib; trap grade
Finish: Blued; engraving; checkered pistol grip stock & forearm; made in five grades; estimated value is for standard grade
Estimated Value: $825.00 - $1,100.00

Ithaca Victory

Ithaca

Ithaca Hammerless Double Field Grade

Gauge: 12, 16, 20, 28, or 410
Action: Box lock; top lever, break-open; hammerless
Magazine: None
Barrel: Double barrel (side by side); 26", 28", 30", or 32"; various choke combinations
Finish: Blued; checkered walnut pistol grip stock & short tapered forearm; made in eight grades; Priced here for Standard Grade; add $50.00 for automatic ejectors, magnum or ventilated rib
Estimated Value: $400.00 - $550.00

Ithaca Hammerless Double Field Grade

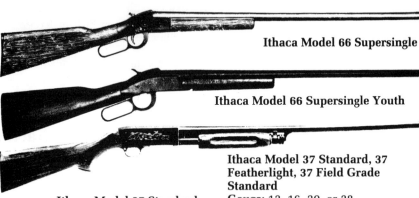

Ithaca Model 66 Supersingle

Ithaca Model 66 Supersingle Youth

Ithaca Model 37 Standard

Ithaca Model 66 Supersingle

Gauge: 20 or 410
Action: Lever action; exposed hammer; single shot
Magazine: None
Barrel: 26", 28", or 30"; full or modified choke
Finish: Blued; plain or checkered straight stock & forearm
Estimated Value: $70.00 - $90.00

Ithaca Model 66 Supersingle Youth

Similar to the 66 except: shorter stock; 410 gauge; 25" barrel; recoil pad
Estimated Value: $65.00 - $85.00

Ithaca Model 37 Standard, 37 Featherlight, 37 Field Grade Standard

Gauge: 12, 16, 20, or 28
Action: Slide action; hammerless; repeating; bottom ejection
Magazine: 4-shot tubular
Barrel: 26", 28", or 30" various chokes
Finish: Blued; walnut, semi-pistol grip stock & grooved or checkered slide handle; add 25% for magnum with interchangeable choke tubes
Estimated Value: $185.00 - $250.00

Ithaca Model 37V, 37 Featherlight Vent, 37 Field Grade Vent

Similar to the Model 37 except: ventilated rib; three interchangeable choke tubes
Estimated Value: $240.00 - $320.00

Ithaca Model 37R

Ithaca Model 37D Deluxe
Similar to the 37 except: checkered
stock & slide handle
Estimated Value: $200.00 - $260.00

Ithaca Model 37R Deluxe
Similar to the 37 Deluxe with a
raised solid rib
Estimated Value: $225.00 - $300.00

Ithaca Model 37DV Deluxe Vent
Similar to the 37D Deluxe except:
ventilated rib
Estimated Value: $310.00 - $390.00

Ithaca Model 37T Trap
Similar to the 37S with trap stock;
recoil pad; choice wood
Estimated Value: $230.00 - $300.00

Ithaca Model 37R
Similar to the 37 with a solid raised
rib; slightly heavier
Estimated Value: $220.00 - $275.00

**Ithaca Model 37 Supreme,
37 Featherlight Supreme,**
Similar to the 37T Target
Estimated Value: $490.00 - $615.00

Ithaca Model 37 Deerslayer

Ithaca Model 37S Skeet
Similar to the 37 with extended
slide handle & ventilated rib
Estimated Value: $225.00 - $300.00

Ithaca Model 37 Deerslayer
Similar to the Model 37 except: 20"
or 25" barrel; rifle sights; 12 or 20
gauge
Estimated Value: $255.00 - $320.00

Ithaca Model 37T Target
Available in skeet or trap version
with high-quality finish & select
wood. Replaced the 37S & 37T Trap
Estimated Value: $245.00 - $325.00

**Ithaca Model 37
Deerslayer Super Deluxe**
Similar to the Model 37 Deerslayer
with higher quality wood & finish
Estimated Value: $275.00 - $350.00

Ithaca

Ithaca Model 37 M&P

Ithaca Model 37 M&P, 87 M&P
Similar to the Model 37 except: for law enforcement use; 18" or 20" cylinder bore barrel; non-glare tung oil finish wood; parkerized or chrome finish metal; add 10% for chrome ; 5 or 8-shot magazine; add 7% for hand grip
Estimated Value: $200.00 - $250.00

Ithaca Model 37 DSPS, DSPS II
A law enforcement version of the Model 37 Deerslayer; grooved slide handle; regular, parkerized, or chrome finished; add 15% for chrome finish; add 5% for 8-shot magazine; deduct 5% for DSPS II
Estimated Value: $200.00 - $250.00

Ithaca Bear Stopper
A short barrel version of the Model 37; 18½" or 20" barrel; 12 gauge; one-hand grip; grooved slide handle; 5 or 8-shot magazine; add 5% for 8-shot; blued or chrome finish; add 10% for chrome
Estimated Value: $225.00 - $300.00

Ithaca Model 37 Ultra Deerslayer,
Similar to the Ultra Featherlight except: 20" barrel for slugs; sights; recoil pad; swivels
Estimated Value: $250.00 - $315.00

Ithaca Model 37 Camo Vent
Similar to the Model 37 Field Grade Vent except: rust-resistant camo finish in spring (green) or fall (brown); sling & swivels; 12 gauge; 26" or 28" full choke barrel
Estimated Value: $330.00 - $410.00

Ithaca Model 37 Ultra Featherlight

Ithaca Model 37
English-Ultra Featherlight
Gauge: 12 or 20
Action: Slide action; hammerless; repeating; aluminum receiver
Magazine: 3-shot tubular
Barrel: 25" full, modified or improved cylinder bore; ventilated rib
Finish: Blued; checkered walnut straight grip stock & slide handle; waterfowl scene on receiver
Estimated Value: $290.00 - $365.00

Ithaca Model 37 Basic Featherlight
Similar to the Model 37 except: without cosmetic finish; no checkering; wood finished in non-glare tung oil; grooved slide handle; "vapor blasted" metal surfaces with a non-glare finish; add 2% for ventilated rib; add 30% for magnum
Estimated Value: $200.00 - $260.00

Ithaca Model 37 & 87
Ultra Featherlight
A 20 gauge lightweight version of the Model 37; aluminum receiver; 25" barrel with ventilated rib; recoil pad; gold plated trigger; interchangeable choke tubes on model 87
Estimated Value: $260.00 - $320.00

Ithaca Model 87 Field

Ithaca Model 87 Ultra Field
Same as Model 87 Field except:
aluminum receiver
Estimated Value: $260.00 - $320.00

Ithaca Model 87 Field
Gauge: 12 or 20
Action: Slide action; hammerless;
repeating
Magazine: 3-shot tubular
Barrel: 26", 28", or 30"; three choke
tubes; 3" chamber; ventilated rib
Finish: Blued; pressed checkered
American walnut stock & side
handle
Estimated Value: $275.00 - $345.00

Ithaca Model 87 Camo Field
Same as Model 87 Field except: 12
gauge with 28" barrel; smooth
American walnut stock & grooved
slide handle; camouflaged finish
Estimated Value: $315.00 - $395.00

Ithaca Model 87 M&P & 87DSPS
Same as Model 87 Field except: 12
gauge with 20" plain barrel; dull oil
finished wood; parkerized or nickel
finish metal; add 25% for nickel
finish; 5 or 8-shot magazine;
cylinder choke
Estimated Value: $245.00 - $300.00

Ithaca Model 87 Deluxe
Same as Model 87 Field except: cut
checkered stock & slide handle with
a high gloss finish & gold plated
trigger
Estimated Value: $300.00 - $370.00

Ithaca Model 87 Supreme
Same as Model 87 Field except: high
grade finish & checkering; gold
plated trigger; Raybar irridescent
orange front sight
Estimated Value: $490.00 - $610.00

Ithaca Model 87 Turkey
Same as Model 87 Field except: 12
gauge with 24" barrel; smooth stock
& slide handle; full choke barrel or
full choke tube; matte blue barrel
with oil finished wood or
camouflaged finish; add $10.00 for
extra choke tube; add 25% for
camouflaged finish
Estimated Value: $250.00 - $315.00

Ithaca

Ithaca Model 87 Deerslayer II

Ithaca Model English 87
Same as model 37 English Ultra Featherlight except: 20 gauge only; 24" or 26" barrel; 3 changeable choke tubes; steel receiver
Estimated Value: $295.00 - $370.00

Ithaca Model 87 Deerslayer
Same as Model 87 Field except: 20" or 25" special bore plain barrel for rifled slugs; 12 gauge only; smooth oil finished stock & grooved slide handle; plain matte finished barrel
Estimated Value: $235.00 - $290.00

Ithaca Model 87 Deerslayer II
Same as Model 87 Deluxe Deerslayer except: Monte Carlo stock; rifled barrel is permanently screwed into the receiver.
Estimated Value: $315.00 - $390.00

Ithaca Model 87 Deluxe Deerslayer
Same as Model 87 Field except: 20" or 25" barrel; cut checkering with high gloss finish; plain barrel with Raybar front sight & adjustable rear; gold plated trigger; special bore; slug barrel or rifled barrel; add 8% for rifled barrel
Estimated Value: $255.00 - $320.00

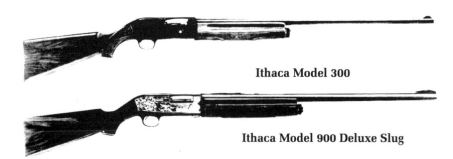

Ithaca Model 300

Ithaca Model 900 Deluxe Slug

Ithaca Model 300
Gauge: 12 or 20
Action: Semi-automatic; recoil operated; hammerless
Magazine: 3-shot tubular
Barrel: 26" improved cylinder; 28" modified or full, 30" full choke; ventilated rib optional; add $10.00 for ventilated rib
Finish: Blued; checkered walnut pistol grip stock & forearm
Estimated Value: $200.00 - $250.00

Ithaca Model 900 Deluxe
Similar to the 300 except: ventilated rib; gold-filled engraving; nameplate in stock; gold-plated trigger
Estimated Value: $240.00 - $300.00

Ithaca Model 900 Deluxe Slug
Similar to the 900 Deluxe except: 24" barrel for slugs; rifle sights
Estimated Value: $245.00 - $310.00

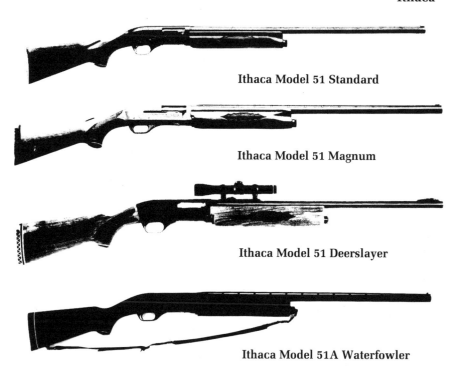

Ithaca Model 51 Standard

Ithaca Model 51 Magnum

Ithaca Model 51 Deerslayer

Ithaca Model 51A Waterfowler

**Ithaca Model 51 Standard,
51 Featherlight, 51A**
Gauge: 12 or 20
Action: Gas operated, semi-automatic
Magazine: 3-shot tubular
Barrel: 26", 28", or 30"; various chokes; ventilated rib optional; add 5% for ventilated rib
Finish: Blued; checkered walnut pistol grip stock & forearm; decorated receiver
Estimated Value: $260.00 - $350.00

Ithaca Model 51 Magnum
Similar to the 51 but chambered for magnum shells; ventilated rib
Estimated Value: $310.00 - $390.00

Ithaca Model 51 Deerslayer
Similar to the Model 51 except: 24" barrel for slugs; sights; recoil pad; 12 gauge only
Estimated Value: $260.00 - $350.00

Ithaca Model 51A Waterfowler, 51A Turkey Gun
Similar to the Model 51A except: matte-finish metal & flat-finish walnut; optional camo finish; add 10% for camo finish; The Turkey model has a 26" ventilated rib barrel, the Waterfowler has a 30" ventilated rib barrel.
Estimated Value: $350.00 - $465.00

Ithaca

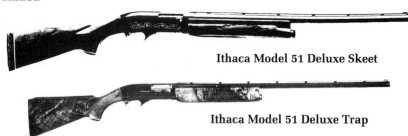

Ithaca Model 51 Deluxe Skeet

Ithaca Model 51 Deluxe Trap

Ithaca Model 51 Deluxe Skeet, 51A Supreme Skeet
Similar to the 51 with recoil pad; ventilated rib; 26", 28", or 29" skeet choke barrel
Estimated Value: $480.00 - $645.00

Ithaca Model 51 Deluxe Trap, 51A Supreme Trap
Similar to the Model 51 except: 12 gauge only; select wood; 28" or 30" barrel; recoil pad; add 5% for Monte Carlo stock
Estimated Value: $490.00 - $650.00

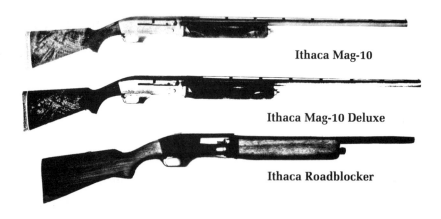

Ithaca Mag-10

Ithaca Mag-10 Deluxe

Ithaca Roadblocker

Ithaca Mag-10 Standard or Deluxe
Gauge: 10 magnum
Action: Semi-automatic; gas operated
Magazine: 3-shot tubular
Barrel: 32" full choke; ventilated rib (deluxe model)
Finish: Blued; plain (standard model) or checkered walnut pistol grip stock & forearm; recoil pad; swivels; deduct 15% for Ithaca Mag-10 Standard
Estimated Value: $525.00 - $700.00

Ithaca Mag-10 Supreme
Similar to the Magnum 10 Deluxe with higher quality finish & select wood
Estimated Value: $630.00 - $840.00

Ithaca Mag-10 Roadblocker
A law enforcement version of the Mag-10 with a 20" barrel; plain stock & forearm; "vapor blasted" metal finish; add 5% for ventilated rib
Estimated Value: $420.00 - $560.00

Iver Johnson

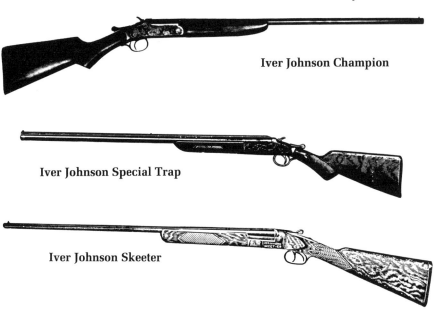

Iver Johnson Champion

Iver Johnson Special Trap

Iver Johnson Skeeter

Iver Johnson Champion
Gauge: 12, 20, or 410
Action: Box lock; top lever, break-open; hammerless; single shot; automatic ejector
Magazine: None
Barrel: 26", 28", or 30"; full choke
Finish: Blued; hardwood semi-pistol grip stock & short tapered forearm
Estimated Value: $85.00 - $110.00

Iver Johnson Special Trap
Similar to the Champion with a 32" ribbed barrel; checkered stock; 12 gauge only
Estimated Value: $150.00 - $190.00

Iver Johnson Matted Rib
Similar to the Champion with a matted rib & checkering
Estimated Value: $110.00 - $135.00

Iver Johnson Hercules
Gauge: 12, 16, 20, or 410
Action: Box lock; top lever, break-open; hammerless; single trigger & automatic ejectors optional; add $75.00 for single trigger or automatic ejectors
Magazine: None
Barrel: Double barrel (side by side); 26", 28", 30", or 32" modified & full or full & full chokes
Finish: Blued; checkered walnut pistol grip stock & tapered forearm
Estimated Value: $320.00 - $400.00

Iver Johnson Skeeter
Similar to the Hercules with addition of 28 gauge; 26" or 28" barrels; wide forearm; add $75.00 for single selective trigger or automatic ejectors
Estimated Value: $400.00 - $500.00

Iver Johnson/Kessler

Iver Johnson Silver Shadow

Iver Johnson Super Trap

Iver Johnson Silver Shadow
Gauge: 12
Action: Box lock; top lever, break-open; hammerless; single trigger optional; add $75.00 for single trigger
Magazine: None
Barrel: Over & under double barrel; 28" modified & full choke; ventilated rib
Finish: Blued; checkered walnut pistol grip stock & forearm
Estimated Value: $300.00 - $375.00

Iver Johnson Super Trap
Gauge: 12
Action: Box lock; top lever, break-open; hammerless; non-selective or selective single trigger or automatic ejectors optional; add $35.00 for non-selective single trigger; $75.00 for selective single trigger or automatic ejectors
Magazine: None
Barrel: Double barrel (side by side); 32" full choke; ventilated rib
Finish: Blued; checkered walnut pistol grip stock & forearm; recoil pad
Estimated Value: $450.00 - $575.00

Kessler

Kessler Lever Matic
Gauge: 12, 16, or 20
Action: Lever action
Magazine: 3-shot
Barrel: 26", 28", or 30"; full choke
Finish: Blued; checkered walnut straight stock & forearm; recoil pad
Estimated Value: $150.00 - $185.00

Kessler 3-Shot
Gauge: 12, 16, or 20
Action: Bolt action; hammerless; repeating
Magazine: 2-shot detachable box
Barrel: 26" or 28"; full choke
Finish: Blued; plain pistol grip stock & forearm, recoil pad
Estimated Value: $75.00 - $95.00

Kleinguenther

Kleinguenther Condor

Kleinguenther Condor Skeet
A skeet version of the Condor with a wide rib
Estimated Value: $500.00 - $625.00

Kleinguenther Condor Trap
A trap version of the Condor with a Monte Carlo stock; wide rib; 32" barrel available
Estimated Value: $510.00 - $640.00

Kleinguenther Condor
Gauge: 12 or 20
Action: Double lock; top lever break-open; hammerless; selective single trigger; automatic ejectors
Magazine: None
Barrel: Over & under double barrel; ventilated rib; 26" improved & modified or skeet; 28" modified or modified & full; 30" modified & full or full in 12 gauge
Finish: Blued; checkered walnut pistol grip stock & forearm; recoil pad
Estimated Value: $480.00 - $600.00

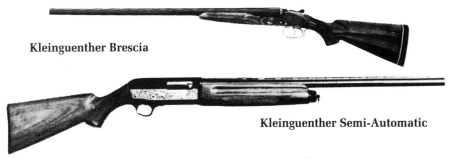

Kleinguenther Brescia

Kleinguenther Semi-Automatic

Kleinguenther Brescia
Gauge: 12 or 20
Action: Box lock; top lever, break-open; hammerless; double trigger
Magazine: None
Barrel: Double barrel (side by side); chrome lined; 28" improved or modified or modified & full chokes
Finish: Blued; checkered walnut pistol grip stock & tapered forearm
Estimated Value: $240.00 - $300.00

Kleinguenther Semi-Automatic
Gauge: 12
Action: Semi-auto; hammerless; side ejection
Magazine: 3-shot tubular
Barrel: Chrome lined; 25" skeet, 26" improved cylinder, 28" & 30" full chokes; ventilated rib
Finish: Blued; smooth walnut pistol grip stock & grooved forearm; engraved
Estimated Value: $260.00 - $325.00

L.C. Smith

**L.C. Smith Double Barrel
(Hunter Arms)**

L.C. Smith Single Barrel
Gauge: 12
Action: Box lock; top lever, break-open; automatic ejectors; hammerless
Magazine: None, single shot
Barrel: 32" or 34"; choice of bore; ventilated rib
Finish: Blued; checkered walnut pistol grip stock & forearm; recoil pad
Estimated Value:
  Olympic: $1,050.00 - $1,500.00
  Specialty: $1,450.00 - $2,000.00
  Crown: $2,500.00 - $3,200.00

L.C. Smith Double Barrel (Hunter Arms)
Gauge: 12, 16, 20, or 410
Action: Side lock, top lever breakdown; hammerless; automatic ejectors; double or single trigger; add $50.00 for single trigger
Magazine: None
Barrel: 26", 28", 30", or 32"; double barrel (side by side) any choke combination
Finish: checkered walnut pistol, semi-pistol grip or straight grip stock & forearm; blued barrels; prices are for Field Grade made by Hunter Arms; other grades higher due to quality of workmanship & finish
Estimated Value: $650.00 - $800.00

L.C. Smith Field Grade (Marlin)

L.C. Smith Field Grade (Marlin)
Same as the Deluxe Model with standard checkered walnut pistol grip stock & forearm; extruded ventilated rib
Estimated Value: $400.00 - $500.00

L.C. Smith Deluxe (Marlin)
Gauge: 12, regular or magnum
Action: Top lever break-open; hammerless; side lock; double triggers
Magazine: None
Barrel: Double barrel (side by side); 28" modified & full chokes; floating steel ventilated rib
Finish: Top quality, hand-fitted, hand-checkered walnut pistol grip stock & beavertail forearm; blued; case hardened side plates
Estimated Value: $415.00 - $520.00

Lefever

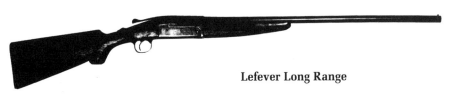

Lefever Long Range

Lefever Long Range
Gauge: 12, 16, 20, or 410
Action: Box lock, top lever, break-open; hammerless; single shot
Magazine: None
Barrel: 26", 28", 30", or 32"; any choke
Finish: Blued; plain or checkered walnut pistol grip stock & forearm
Estimated Value: $180.00 - $225.00

Lefever Trap
Gauge: 12
Action: Box lock; top lever break-open; hammerless; single shot
Magazine: None
Barrel: 30" or 32" full choke; ventilated rib
Finish: Blued; checkered walnut pistol grip stock & forearm; recoil pad
Estimated Value: $360.00 - $450.00

Lefever Trap

Lefever Nitro Special

Lefever Excellsior
Similar to Nitro-Special with light engraving & automatic ejectors
Estimated Value: $460.00 - $575.00

Lefever Nitro Special
Gauge: 12, 16, 20, or 410
Action: Box lock; top lever, break-open; hammerless; double triggers; single trigger optional; add $75.00 for single trigger
Magazine: None
Barrel: Double barrel (side by side); 26", 28", 30", or 32"; any choke
Finish: Blued; checkered walnut pistol grip stock & forearm
Estimated Value: $440.00 - $550.00

Mannlicher

Mannlicher Gamba Oxford

Mannlicher Gamba Oxford
Gauge: 12, 20, or 20; regular or magnum
Action: Top lever break-open; hammerless; single or double trigger; add $140.00 for single trigger
Magazine: None
Barrel: Double barrel (side by side); 26½" improved cylinder & modified or 27½" modified & full
Finish: Blued; engraved receiver; checkered walnut straight grip stock & tapered forearm
Estimated Value: $995.00 - $1,325.00

Mannlicher Gamba Principessa
Gauge: 28
Action: Top lever break-open; hammerless; single or double trigger; add $130.00 for single trigger
Magazine: None
Barrel: Double barrel (side by side); 26" improved cylinder & modified or 28" modified & full
Finish: Blued; case hardened receiver with engraved scrollwork; checkered walnut straight grip stock & tapered forearm
Estimated Value: $880.00 - $1,175.00

Marlin

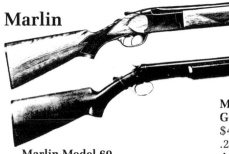

Marlin Model 90

Marlin Model 60

Marlin Model 60
Gauge: 12
Action: Box lock; top lever, break-open; exposed hammer; single shot
Magazine: None
Barrel: 30" or 32" full choke; matted top; 2¾" chamber
Finish: Blued; walnut pistol grip stock & beavertail forearm
Estimated Value: $145.00 - $185.00

Marlin Model 90
Gauge: 12, 16, 20, or 410; add $40.00 for 410 gauge; also .22 & .222 calibers
Action: Top lever break-open; box lock; double trigger; single trigger optional; add $50.00 for single trigger; hammerless
Magazine: None
Barrel: Over & under double barrel, 26", 28", or 30" rifle; 26" shotgun barrels; 2¾" chamber, 3" chamber in 410; full, modified, skeet or improved cylinder bore
Finish: Blued; plain or checkered walnut pistol grip stock & forearm; recoil pad
Estimated Value: $350.00 - $440.00

Marlin Model 410

Marlin Model 55 Hunter

Marlin Model 410
Gauge: 410
Action: Lever action; exposed hammer
Magazine: 5-shot tubular
Barrel: 22" or 26", 2½" chamber
Finish: Blued; walnut pistol grip stock & beavertail forearm
Estimated Value: $375.00 - $470.00

Marlin Model 55 Hunter
Gauge: 12, 16, or 20
Action: Bolt action; repeating
Magazine: 2-shot clip
Barrel: 26" or 28" full choke; also "Micro Choke;" 2¾" or 3" chamber
Finish: Blued; walnut pistol grip stock & forearm
Estimated Value: $80.00 - $100.00

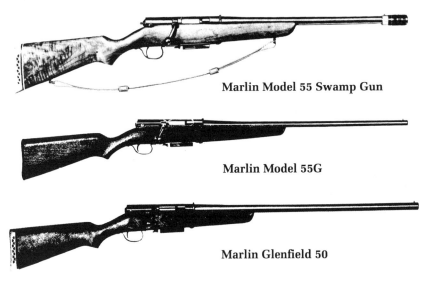

Marlin Model 55 Swamp Gun

Marlin Model 55G

Marlin Glenfield 50

Marlin Model 55 Swamp Gun
Same as the Model 55 except: shorter barrel with "Micro Choke;" recoil pad & swivels; chambered for 3" 12 gauge magnum shells
Estimated Value: $80.00 - $100.00

Marlin 55G, Glenfield 55G & Glenfield 50
Similar to the Marlin Model 55 Hunter; it was produced from about 1961 to 1966 as the 55G & Glenfield 55G, & in 1966 it became the Glenfield 50.
Estimated Value: $75.00 - $95.00

Marlin

Marlin Model 55S Slug Gun

Marlin Model 55 Goose Gun

Marlin Model 59

Marlin Glenfield 60G

Marlin Model 59, 60G, 61G
Gauge: 410
Action: Bolt action
Magazine: None; single shot
Barrel: 24" full coke; chambered for 2½" or 3" shells
Finish: Blued; walnut pistol grip or semi-pistol grip stock & forearm
Estimated Value: $70.00 - $90.00

Marlin Model 55S Slug Gun
Similar to the Model 55 except: rifle sights; 24" barrel; chambered for 2¾" & 3" shells; swivels & recoil pad
Estimated Value: $75.00 - $100.00

Marlin Model 5510 Supergoose 10
Gauge: 10 gauge magnum
Action: Bolt action
Magazine: 2-shot clip (2⅞" shells must be loaded singly)
Barrel: 34" full choke; chambered for 3½" shells
Finish: Blued; black walnut semi-pistol grip stock & forearm; swivels; recoil pad
Estimated Value: $165.00 - $210.00

Marlin Model 55 Goose Gun
Same as the Model 55 except: swivels; extra long 36" barrel; chambered for 3" 12 gauge magnum shells; recoil pad
Estimated Value: $160.00 - $200.00

Pocket Guide to Shotguns

Marlin Model 19

Marlin Model 1898

Marlin Model 1898
Gauge: 12 (2¾")
Action: Slide action; exposed hammer; side ejection
Magazine: 5-shot tubular
Barrel: 26", 28", 30", or 32"
Finish: Blued; walnut pistol grip stock & grooved slide handle; produced in many grades from 1898 to 1905; price for Grade A (Field Grade)
Estimated Value: $315.00 - $390.00

Marlin Model 19 & 19G
Similar to the Model 1898 with improvements; Model 19 made from 1906 to 1907; 19G produced until 1915
Estimated Value: $260.00 - $325.00

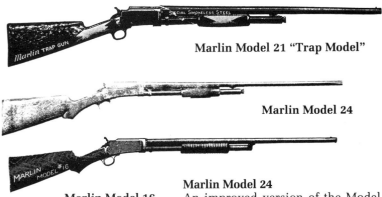

Marlin Model 21 "Trap Model"

Marlin Model 24

Marlin Model 16

Marlin Model 24
An improved version of the Model 19 made from 1908 to 1915
Estimated Value: $270.00 - $355.00

Marlin Model 21 "Trap Model"
Similar to the Model 24 with trap specifications. Made from 1907 to 1909
Estimated Value: $275.00 - $345.00

Marlin Model 16
Gauge: 16 (2¾")
Action: Slide action; exposed hammer
Magazine: 5-shot tubular
Barrel: 26" or 28"
Finish: Blued; walnut pistol grip stock & forearm; some checkered, some with grooved slide handle
Estimated Value: $280.00 - $355.00

Marlin Model 26
Similar to the Model 24 except: straight grip stock; solid frame
Estimated Value: $260.00 - $325.00

Marlin

Marlin Model 28

Marlin Model 28T

Marlin Model 28A

Marlin Model 31

Marlin Model 31A

Marlin Model 28, 28T, 28TS
Gauge: 12
Action: Slide action; hammerless; side ejection
Magazine: 5-shot tubular
Barrel: 26" or 28" cylinder bore or modified choke; 30" or 32" full choke
Finish: Blued; checkered walnut pistol grip stock & slide handle; the Models 28T & 28TS were Trap Grade guns with an available straight stock; add $100.00 for 28T or 28TS
Estimated Value: $280.00 - $350.00

Marlin Model 28A
Similar to the Model 28; made from about 1920 to 1922; replaced by the Model 43A
Estimated Value: $265.00 - $330.00

Marlin Model 31
Similar to the Model 28 except: 20 or 16 gauge; made from about 1915 to 1917 & 1920 to 1922
Estimated Value: $270.00 - $360.00

Marlin Model 31A
Similar to the Model 28A except: 20 gauge only; replaced by the Model 44A
Estimated Value: $265.00 - $350.00

Pocket Guide to Shotguns

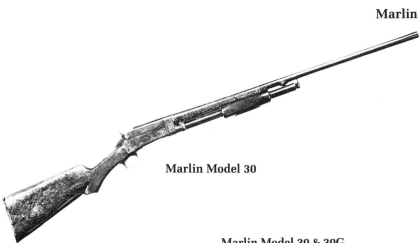

Marlin Model 30

Marlin Model 17 & 17G
Gauge: 12
Action: Slide action; exposed hammer
Magazine: 5-shot tubular
Barrel: 30" or 32" full choke; other chokes available by special order
Finish: Blued; walnut pistol grip stock & grooved slide handle; after 1908 as Model 17G
Estimated Value: $265.00 - $330.00

Marlin Model 30 & 30G
Gauge: 16 or 20
Action: Slide action; exposed hammer
Magazine: 5-shot tubular
Barrel: 25", 26", or 28" modified choke, 2¾" chamber
Finish: Blued; checkered walnut straight or pistol grip stock, grooved or checkered slide handle; after 1915 it was called the Model 30G
Estimated Value: $235.00 - $295.00

Marlin Model 42A

Marlin Model 49
Similar to the Model 42A. It was given away with stock in the corporation. Produced from about 1925 to 1928
Estimated Value: $275.00 - $375.00

Marlin Model 42A
Gauge: 12
Action: Slide action; exposed hammer; side ejection
Magazine: 5-shot tubular; bottom load
Barrel: 26" cylinder bore, 28" modified, 30" & 32" full choke; 2¾" chamber; round matted barrel
Finish: Blued; black walnut semi-pistol grip stock; grooved slide handle
Estimated Value: $230.00 - $290.00

Marlin

Marlin Model 43A

Marlin Model 43T

Marlin Model 44A

Marlin Model 43A
Gauge: 12
Action: Slide action; hammerless; side ejection
Magazine: 5-shot tubular
Barrel: 26" cylinder bore, 28" modified, 30" & 32" full choke; 2¾" chamber
Finish: Blued; walnut pistol grip stock & grooved slide handle
Estimated Value: $200.00 - $250.00

Marlin Model 43T & 43TS
Same basic shotgun as the Model 43A except: checkered Monte Carlo stock & forearm with recoil pad; the Model 43TS had a choice of many options, & the value is dependent on the number & type of extras.
Estimated Value: $300.00 - $375.00

Marlin Model 53
Similar to Model 43A; made in Standard Grade only; replaced by Model 63A
Estimated Value: $280.00 - $350.00

Marlin Model 44A
Gauge: 20
Action: Slide action; hammerless; side ejection
Magazine: 4-shot tubular; bottom load
Barrel: 25" or 28"; cylinder bore, modified or full choke; 2¾" chamber
Finish: Blued; walnut pistol grip stock & grooved slide handle
Estimated Value: $285.00 - $360.00

Marlin Model 44S
Same basic shotgun as the Model 44A except: straight or pistol grip checkered stock & forearm
Estimated Value: $295.00 - $370.00

Marlin Model 63A
Gauge: 12
Action: Slide action; hammerless; side ejector
Magazine: 5-shot tubular
Barrel: 26" cylinder bore, 28" modified choke, 30" or 32" full choke
Finish: Blued; plain walnut pistol grip stock & grooved slide handle; improved version of the Model 43A
Estimated Value: $200.00 - $275.00

Marlin Model 63T & 63TS
Similar to the Model 63A except: trap version; 30" or 32" barrel; checkered straight stock; the Model 63TS could be ordered to the buyer's specifications; prices are for Standard Trap gun
Estimated Value: $240.00 - $325.00

Marlin Model Premier Mark I

Marlin Model Premier Mark II

Marlin Model Premier Mark IV

Marlin Model Premier Mark I
Gauge: 12
Action: Slide action; hammerless; side ejection
Magazine: 3-shot tubular
Barrel: 26" cylinder bore, 28" modified, 30" full choke; ventilated rib optional; also 28" slug barrel with rifle sights; 2¾" chamber
Finish: Blued; walnut pistol grip stock & forearm; recoil pad optional
Estimated Value: $135.00 - $170.00

Marlin Model Premier Mark II
Same as the Premier Mark I except: stock & forearm are checkered & receiver is engraved
Estimated Value: $165.00 - $210.00

Marlin Model Premier Mark IV
Same as the Mark II except: the wood is more elaborate & the engraving heavier
Estimated Value: $230.00 - $290.00

Marlin

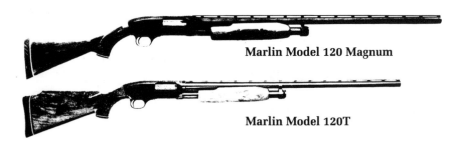

Marlin Model 120 Magnum

Marlin Model 120T

Marlin Deluxe 120 Slug Gun
Similar to the Marlin 120 except: 20"
slug barrel & rifle sights
Estimated Value: $230.00 - $290.00

Marlin Model 120T
Same as Model 120 with a Monte
Carlo stock & 30" full choke or 30"
modified trap choke barrel
Estimated Value: $240.00 - $300.00

Marlin Model 120 Magnum
Gauge: 12 gauge magnum
Action: Slide action; hammerless
Magazine: 5-shot tubular (4-shot
with 3" shells)
Barrel: 26" cylinder bore, 28"
modified or 30" full choke; also 26"
choked slug barrel
Finish: Blued; ventilated rib;
checkered walnut, pistol grip stock
& forearm; recoil pad
Estimated Value: $225.00 - $280.00

Marlin Glenfield 778

Marlin Glenfield 778 Slug
Same as the Glenfield 778 except:
20" slug barrel & rifle sights
Estimated Value: $150.00 - $200.00

Marlin Glenfield 778
Gauge: 12, regular or magnum
Action: Slide action; hammerless;
repeating
Magazine: 5-shot tubular; 4-shot for
3" magnum
Barrel: 26" improved cylinder; 28"
modified; 30" full choke; ventilated
rib optional; add $50.00 for
ventilated rib; 38" MXR full choke
barrel available without rib
Finish: Blued; checkered hardwood,
semi-pistol grip stock & fluted slide
handle; recoil pad
Estimated Value: $145.00 - $180.00

Mauser

Mauser Model 496 Trap

Mauser Model 496 Competition

Mauser Model 496 Competition
Same as the Model 496 except: select wood; higher ventilated rib
Estimated Value: $540.00 - $675.00

Mauser Model 496 Trap
Gauge: 12
Action: Box lock; top lever, break-open; hammerless; single shot
Magazine: None
Barrel: 32" modified or 34" full choke; ventilated rib
Finish: Blued; checkered walnut Monte Carlo pistol grip stock & tapered forearm; engraved; recoil pad
Estimated Value: $440.00 - $550.00

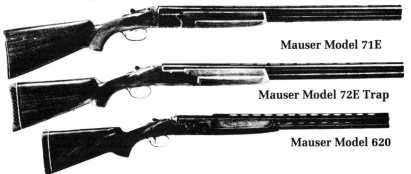

Mauser Model 71E

Mauser Model 72E Trap

Mauser Model 620

Mauser Model 71E
Similar to the Model 620 except: double triggers & no recoil pad; 28" barrel
Estimated Value: $380.00 - $475.00

Mauser Model 72E Trap
Similar to the Model 71E except: large recoil pad; engraving; wide high rib; single trigger
Estimated Value: $500.00 - $625.00

Mauser Model 620
Gauge: 12
Action: Box lock; top lever, break-open; hammerless; automatic ejectors; single trigger
Magazine: None
Barrel: Over & under double barrel; 28" or 30" improved cylinder & modified or modified & full or skeet chokes; ventilated rib
Finish: Blued; plain walnut pistol grip stock & forearm; recoil pad
Estimated Value: $760.00 - $950.00

Mauser

Mauser Model 580

Mauser Model 580
Gauge: 12
Action: Side lock; top lever break-open; hammerless
Magazine: None
Barrel: Double barrel (side by side); 28" or 30", various choke combinations
Finish: Blued; checkered walnut straight stock & tapered forearm; engraved
Estimated Value: $720.00 - $900.00

Mauser Model 610 Phantom

Mauser Model 610 Phantom
Gauge: 12
Action: Box lock; top lever, break-open; hammerless
Magazine: None
Barrel: Over & under double barrel; ventilated rib between barrels & on top of barrel; 30" or 32" various choke combinations
Finish: Blued; case hardened receiver; checkered walnut pistol grip stock & forearm; recoil pad
Estimated Value: $780.00 - $975.00

Mauser Contest
Gauge: 12
Action: Top lever, break-open; automatic ejectors; single selective trigger
Magazine: None
Barrel: Over & under double barrel; 27½" improved cylinder & improved modified
Finish: Blued; engraved gray sideplates; checkered walnut pistol grip stock & lipped forearm
Estimated Value: 840.00 - $1,050.00

Mossberg

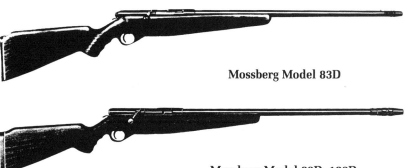

Mossberg Model 83D

Mossberg Model 183K

Mossberg Model 83D, 183D
Gauge: 410
Action: Bolt action; repeating
Magazine: 2-shot, top loading, fixed magazine
Barrel: 23" on 83D, 24" on 183D; interchangeable choke fittings
Finish: Blued; hardwood Monte Carlo semi-pistol grip one-piece stock & forearm; after 1948 called 183D
Estimated Value: $75.00 - $95.00

Mossberg Model 183K
Same as 183D except: adjustable choke & recoil pad
Estimated Value: $80.00 - $110.00

Mossberg Model 185K

Mossberg Model 190K

Mossberg Model 190K
Same as 183K except: 16 gauge
Estimated Value: $75.00 - $95.00

Mossberg Model 185K
Same as 183K except: 20 gauge
Estimated Value: $80.00 - $100.00

Mossberg Model 195K
Same as 183K except: 12 gauge
Estimated Value: $85.00 - $105.00

Mossberg

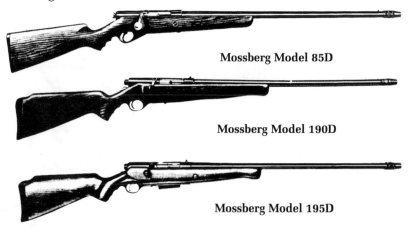

Mossberg Model 85D

Mossberg Model 190D

Mossberg Model 195D

Mossberg Model 190D
Same as 185D except 16 gauge
Estimated Value: $65.00 - $85.00

Mossberg Model 195D
Same as 185D except 12 gauge
Estimated Value: $75.00 - $95.00

Mossberg Model 85D & 185D
Gauge: 20
Action: Bolt action; repeating
Magazine: 2-shot detachable box
Barrel: 25" on 85D, 26" on 185D; interchangeable choke fittings
Finish: Blued; hardwood pistol grip one-piece stock & forearm; called 185D after 1948
Estimated Value: $75.00 - $95.00

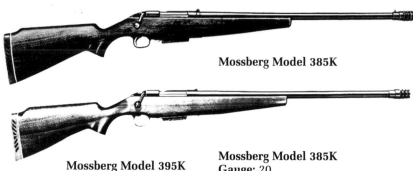

Mossberg Model 385K

Mossberg Model 395K

Mossberg Model 395K
Same as 385K in 12 gauge
Estimated Value: $75.00 - $100.00

Mossberg Model 385K
Gauge: 20
Action: Bolt action; repeating
Magazine: 2-shot detachable box
Barrel: 26" adjustable choke
Finish: Blued; wood Monte Carlo semi-pistol grip one-piece stock & tapered forearm; recoil pad
Estimated Value: $75.00 - $100.00

Mossberg Model 390K

Mossberg Model 585
Similar to the Model 385K with improved safety
Estimated Value: $90.00 - $120.00

Mossberg Model 390 K
Similar to the 385K except: 16 gauge; 28" adjustable choke barrel
Estimated Value: $75.00 - $95.00

Mossberg Model 595
Similar to the Model 395K except: improved safety; 28" adjustable choke barrel
Estimated Value: $90.00 - $120.00

Mossberg Model 395 SPL
Similar to the Model 395K with a 38" full choke waterfowl barrel; swivels
Estimated Value: $100.00 - $125.00

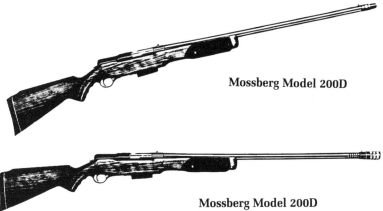

Mossberg Model 200D

Mossberg Model 200K

Mossberg Model 200K
Similar to the 200D with adjustable choke
Estimated Value: $100.00 - $125.00

Mossberg Model 200D
Gauge: 12
Action: Slide action; hammerless; repeating; slide handle is metal cover over wood forearm
Magazine: 3-shot detachable box
Barrel: 28" interchangeable choke fittings
Finish: Blued; wood Monte Carlo semi-pistol grip one-piece stock & forearm
Estimated Value: $90.00 - $115.00

Mossberg

Mossberg Model 3000 Field
Gauge: 12 or 20; regular or magnum
Action: Slide action; hammerless; repeating
Magazine: 4-shot tubular, 3-shot in magnum
Barrel: 26" improved cylinder, 28" modified or full, 30" full; ventilated rib; "Multi-choke" optional; add 10% for "Multi-choke"
Finish: Checkered walnut pistol grip stock & slide handle
Estimated Value: $200.00 - $265.00

Mossberg Model 3000 Waterfowler
Similar to the Model 3000 except: 30" full choke barrel only; parkerized oiled finish or camo finish with "Speedfeed" storage stock; add 10% for "Speedfeed" storage stock or "Multi-choke"
Estimated Value: $215.00 - $290.00

Mossberg Model 3000 Slug
Similar to the Model 3000 except: 22" slug barrel & rifle sights; black finish and "speedfeed storage stock;" add $35.00 for black finish with "Speedfeed" storage stock
Estimated Value: $185.00 - $250.00

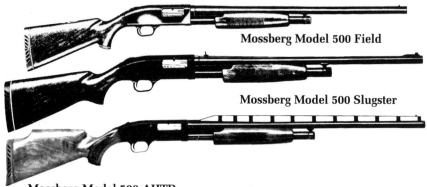

Mossberg Model 500 Field

Mossberg Model 500 Slugster

Mossberg Model 500 AHTD

Mossberg Model 500 Slugster
Similar to 500 field except: 18" or 24" slug barrel & rifle sights; add 20% for removable chokes; add 15% for Trophy Model; add 12% for rifled barrel
Estimated Value: $155.00 - $205.00

Mossberg Model 500 Hi-Rib Trap, AHTD, AHT
Similar to 500 field except: high rib barrel & Monte Carlo stock; AHTD adjustable choke; AHT full choke; 28" or 30" barrel
Estimated Value: $200.00 - $270.00

Mossberg Model 500 Field
Gauge: 12, 16, 20, or 410
Action: Slide action; hammerless; repeating
Magazine: 5-shot tubular
Barrel: 24" in Junior Model; 26" adjustable choke or improved cylinder; 28" modified or full; 30" full choke (12 gauge only); "Accu-Choke" optional; add 3% for "Accu-Choke;" vent rib optional; add 8% for vent rib
Finish: Blued; walnut pistol grip stock & grooved slide handle; recoil pad; optional camo finish & "Speedfeed" stock after 1985 (add 25% for camo finish & "Speedfeed" stock)
Estimated Value: $165.00 - $205.00

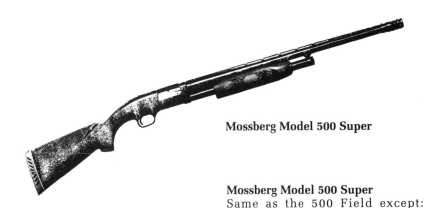

Mossberg Model 500 Super

Mossberg Model 500 Super
Same as the 500 Field except: checkered stock & slide handle; ventilated rib; 12 gauge magnum
Estimated Value: $175.00 - $215.00

Mossberg Model 500 ALDR, CLDR, ALDRX
Similar to 500 field in 12 gauge (ALDR); 20 gauge (CLDR) with removable choke; (ALDRX) slugster barrel
Estimated Value: $160.00 - $200.00

Mossberg Model 500 ALMR Duck Gun
Same as 500 field except: 12 gauge magnum; 30" or 32" vent rib barrel
Estimated Value: $170.00 - $210.00

Mossberg Model 500 Security & Persuader ATP8

Mossberg Model 500 Security & Persuader ATP6
Similar to the Model 500 field except: built in several models for law enforcement use; 12 gauge, 6-shot, 18½" barrel; add 17% for Parkerized finish; add 9% for rifle sights; add 26% for nickel finish; add 13% for "Speedfeed" stock; add 22% for camo finish
Estimated Value: $150.00 - $185.00

Mossberg Model 500 Security & Persuader ATP8
Similar to the Model 500 ATP6 series except: 20" barrel; 8-shot capacity; add 8% for rifle sights; 16% for parkerized finish; 24% for nickel finish; 12% for "Speedfeed" stock; 20% for camo finish
Estimated Value: $150.00 - $185.00

Mossberg

Mossberg Model 500 ER

Mossberg Model 500 Persuader Cruiser
Similar to the Model 500 ATP6 and ATP8 series law enforcement shotguns except: one-hand grip; add 26% for nickel finish
Estimated Value: $145.00 - $180.00

Mossberg Model 500 Mariner
Similar to the Persuader series except: special Teflon & metal coating that is resistant to salt water spray; stock & slide handle are synthetic; 6 or 9-shot; add 20% for 9-shot model; 10% for "Speedfeed" stock
Estimated Value: $200.00 - $250.00

Mossberg Model 500 APR Pigeon
Similar to the 500 Field except: engraving; ventilated rib
Estimated Value: $190.00 - $260.00

Mossberg Model 500 ARTP Trap
Similar to the 500 APR except: 30" full choke barrel; Monte Carlo stock
Estimated Value: $200.00 - $275.00

Mossberg Model 500 Camper
Similar to the Model 500 Persuader Cruiser in 12 gauge, 20 gauge, or 410 bore; 18½" barrel; synthetic grip & slide handle; camo carrying case
Estimated Value: $170.00 - $210.00

Mossberg Model 500 ER, ELR
Similar to the 500 Field except: 410 gauge; 26" barrel; skeet version; checkering & ventilated rib
Estimated Value: $150.00 - $200.00

Mossberg 500 Security & Persuader CTP6, ETP6
Similar to the other 500 series law enforcement shotguns in 20 gauge (CTP6) or 410 bore (ETP6); 18½" barrel; 6-shot
Estimated Value: $150.00 - $190.00

Mossberg Model 500 Regal
Similar to the Model 500 field except: deluxe finish; crown design on receiver; add $20.00 for "Accu-Choke"
Estimated Value: $165.00 - $210.00

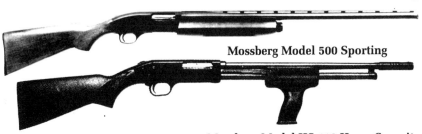

Mossberg Model 500 Sporting

Mossberg Model HS 410 Home Security

Mossberg Model 500 Sporting
Gauge: 12, 20, or 410; regular or magnum
Action: Slide action, hammerless; repeating; double slide bars
Magazine: 5-shot tubular
Barrel: 20", 24", 26", or 28"; "Accu-Choke" tubes or fixed choke; plain or ventilated rib
Finish: Blued or camo; add 8% for camo finish; checkered walnut finish stock and slide handle or synthetic stock and slide handle; add 18% for ghost ring sights
Estimated Value: $165.00 - $205.00

Mossberg Model HS 410 Home Security
Gauge: 410; 3" chamber
Action: Slide action, hammerless; repeating
Magazine: 4-shot tubular
Barrel: 18½" with muzzle brake and spreader choke (the spreader choke delivers almost twice the size circle of a regular shotgun pattern)
Finish: Blued with synthetic stock and slide handle; the laser light sight model has a vertical hand grip slide which contain the light and battery; add 82% for laser light model
Estimated Value: $185.00 - $230.00

Mossberg 835 Camo Ulti-Mag

Mossberg 835 Field Grade Ulti-Mag
Gauge: 12 (3½" chamber); regular or magnum
Action: Slide action, hammerless; repeating; double slide bars
Magazine: 4 or 5-shot tubular
Barrel: 24" or 28"; with ventilated rib; "Accu-Mag" Choke tube or 24" with rifle sights and cylinder bore fixed choke; deduct 4% for 24" fixed cylinder bore choke barrel with rifle sights
Finish: Blued, walnut-finish, checkered stock and slide handle
Estimated Value: $170.00 - $210.00

Mossberg 835 Regal Ulti-Mag
Same as 835 Field Grade Ulti-Mag except: walnut stock and slide handle; dual-comb stock (stock comb height can be changed by removing one bolt); 24" rifle bore barrel with scope base optional; add 5% for 24" rifle bore barrel
Estimated Value: $225.00 - $280.00

Mossberg 835 Camo Ulti-Mag
Same as 835 Regal Ulti-Mag except: camo finish; the National Wild Turkey Federation (NWTF) Model has synthetic stock (without dual comb feature) and slide handle with "Realtree" Camo pattern and 24" barrel with x-full tube Accu-Mag choke; add 7% for the NWTF Model
Estimated Value: $240.00 - $300.00

Mossberg

Mossberg Model 5500

Mossberg Model 5500 Slugster

Mossberg Model 9200

Mossberg Model 9200
Gauge: 12, regular or magnum
Action: Gas operated semi-automatic; a gas regulating system compensates for varied pressures from normal to magnum loads
Magazine: 4-shot; 3-shot in magnum
Barrel: 24" rifled bore; 24" or 28" smooth bore with Accu-Choke tubes; wide ventilated rib, white front bead and brass midpoint bead
Finish: Blued or camo; checkered pistol grip walnut finish stock and forearm; camo finish has synthetic stock and forearm; add 65% for camo finish; the 24" rifled bore has walnut finish dual-comb stock in blued finish; add 6% for 24" rifled bore with dual comb stock
Estimated Value: $225.00 - $280.00

Mossberg Model 5500
Gauge: 12, regular or magnum
Action: Gas operated semi-automatic
Magazine: 4-shot tubular
Barrel: 25" (youth model); 26" improved cylinder, 28" modified, 30" full, or 28" "Accu-Choke" with interchangeable tubes; ventilated rib optional
Finish: Blued; checkered hardwood or synthetic semi-pistol grip stock & forearm; aluminum alloy receiver; youth model has smaller stock
Estimated Value: $225.00 - $280.00

Mossberg Model 5500 Slugster
Similar to the Model 5500 except: 18½" or 24" slug barrel; rifle sights & swivels
Estimated Value: $255.00 - $335.00

Mossberg Model 1000 Field

Mossberg Model 1000 Super Skeet
Similar to the Model 1000 Super
with 25" skeet barrel
Estimated Value: $370.00 - $495.00

Mossberg Model 1000 Super
Gauge: 12 or 20, regular or magnum
Action: Gas operated semi-automatic
Magazine: 3-shot tubular
Barrel: 26", 28", or 30" "Multi-choke;" ventilated rib
Finish: Blued; checkered walnut pistol grip stock & forearm; recoil pad; scrolling on receiver
Estimated Value: $300.00 - $400.00

Mossberg Model 1000 Field
Similar to the Model 1000 Super
except: alloy receiver; various chokes
available including a 26" skeet barrel;
add $30.00 for "Multi-choke;" Junior
model has 22" barrel with "Multi-choke;" add 15% for Junior model
Estimated Value: $245.00 - $330.00

Mossberg Model 1000 Super Waterfowler
Similar to the Model 1000 Super
except: dull wood & Parkerized
finish; 12 gauge only
Estimated Value: $315.00 - $420.00

Mossberg Model 1000 Slug
Similar to the Model 1000 Field
except: 22" slug barrel with rifle
sights
Estimated Value: $240.00 - $320.00

Mossberg Model 1000 Super Slug
Similar to the Model 1000 Super
with 22" slug barrel
Estimated Value: $295.00 - $395.00

Mossberg Model 1000 Trap
Similar to the Model 1000 Field
except: 30" "Multi-choke" barrel,
recoil pad, Monte Carlo stock & high-rib barrel
Estimated Value: $315.00 - $420.00

Mossberg 712 Camo

Mossberg Model 712 Camo
Similar to the Model 712 except:
camo finish & "Speedfeed" storage
stock; add 15% for "Accu-Choke"
Estimated Value: $220.00 - $290.00

Mossberg Model 712 Regal
Same as Model 712 except: deluxe
finish, crown design on receiver;
add 15% for "Accu-Choke"
Estimated Value: $200.00 - $275.00

Mossberg Model 712
Gauge: 12, regular or magnum
Action: Gas operated semi-
automatic; designed to handle any
12 gauge shell interchangeably
Magazine: 4-shot tubular, 3-shot in
magnum
Barrel: 30" full, 28" modified, 24"
"Accu-choke;" add 15% for "Accu-
choke;" 24" slug model; add 8% for
slug model with rifle sights;
ventilated rib optional; add 8% for
ventilated rib
Finish: Alloy receiver with anodized
finish; checkered walnut finish semi-
pistol grip stock & forearm; recoil
pad; Junior Model has 13" stock.
Estimated Value: $205.00 - $260.00

New England

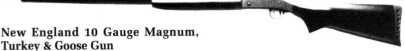

**New England 10 Gauge Magnum,
Turkey & Goose Gun**
Gauge: 10 magnum; 3½" chamber
Action: Side lever release, break-
open; single shot; exposed hammer
Magazine: None, single shot
Barrel: 28" or 32" full choke
Finish: Blued; hardwood walnut
finish, smooth, pistol grip stock &
forearm; recoil pad; also camo matte
finish stock & forearm (after 1991);
add 12% for camo finish
Estimated Value: $105.00 - $130.00

New England 10 Gauge Magnum

New England Turkey
Similar to the 10 gauge magnum
turkey & goose gun except: 24"
barrel; "Mossy oak" or "Bottom
land" camo finish
Estimated Value: $80.00 - $100.00

New England Pardner

New England Deluxe Pardner
Same as the Pardner except: 12 or 20
gauge only; special double back-up
butt stock (holds two spare shells) &
recoil pad
Estimated Value: $95.00 - $120.00

New England Pardner
Gauge: 12, 16, 20, 28, or 410; also
12 magnum
Action: side lever release; break-
open; single shot; exposed hammer
Magazine: None, single shot
Barrel: 24", 26", or 28"; full,
modified, or cylinder bore
Finish: Blued with color case
hardened receiver; hardwood walnut
finish pistol grip, smooth stock &
lipped forearm
Estimated Value: $75.00 - $95.00

New England Mini-Pardner
Same as the Pardner except: 20 or
410 gauge only, 18½" barrel; short
stock; equipped with swivel studs
Estimated Value: $90.00 - $110.00

New England Protector
Gauge: 12
Action: side lever release, break-
open; single shot; exposed hammer
Magazine: None, single shot
Barrel: 18½" plain
Finish: Blued or nickel; add 8% for
nickel finish; smooth hardwood
walnut finish pistol grip stock &
lipped forearm; recoil pad; special
double back-up butt stock holds two
spare shells; swivels
Estimated Value: $100.00 - $125.00

New England Youth Pardner
Same as the Pardner except: 20 or
410 gauge only with 22" barrel &
straight grip, shorter stock with
recoil pad
Estimated Value: $80.00 - $100.00

New Haven

New Haven Model 273

New Haven Model 273
Gauge: 20
Action: Bolt action; hammerless;
single shot
Magazine: None
Barrel: 24" full choke
Finish: Blued; plain walnut Monte
Carlo semi-pistol grip one-piece
stock & forearm
Estimated Value: $60.00 - $75.00

New Haven

New Haven Model 290

New Haven Model 290
Gauge: 16
Action: Bolt action; hammerless; repeating
Magazine: 2-shot detachable box
Barrel: 28"; removable full choke
Finish: Blued; walnut Monte Carlo pistol grip one-piece stock & tapered forearm
Estimated Value: $65.00 - $85.00

New Haven Model 283 or 283T
A 410 gauge version of the 290 with a 24" barrel; also called 283T
Estimated Value: $70.00 - $90.00

New Haven Model 295
A 12 gauge version of the 290
Estimated Value: $60.00 - $80.00

New Haven Model 285
A 20 gauge version of the model 290 with 24" barrel
Estimated Value: $65.00 - $85.00

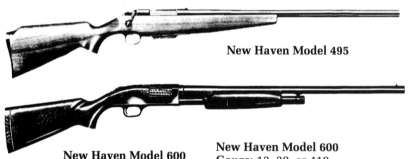

New Haven Model 495

New Haven Model 600

New Haven Model 495, 495T
Gauge: 12
Action: Bolt action; hammerless; repeating
Magazine: 2-shot detachable box
Barrel: 28" full choke
Finish: Blued; walnut Monte Carlo semi-pistol grip stock & tapered forearm
Estimated Value: $85.00 - $110.00

New Haven Model 485T
A 20 gauge version of the Model 495 with 26" barrel
Estimated Value: $90.00 - $120.00

New Haven Model 600
Gauge: 12, 20, or 410
Action: Slide action; hammerless; repeating
Magazine: 6-shot tubular
Barrel: 26" improved cylinder, 28" modified or full, 30" full choke; ventilated rib optional; add 20% for ventilated rib; adjustable choke; add 10% for adjustable choke; changeable choke tubes; add 6% for changeable choke tubes
Finish: Blued; walnut semi-pistol grip stock & slide handle
Estimated Value: $140.00 - $175.00

New Haven Model 600 AST
Similar to Model 600 with 24" barrel & rifle sights
Estimated Value: $145.00 - $180.00

Noble Model 420

Noble Model 420
Gauge: 12, 16, or 20
Action: Box lock; top lever, break-open; hammerless; double triggers
Magazine: None
Barrel: Double barrel (side by side); 28" modified & full choke
Finish: Blued; checkered walnut pistol grip stock & forearm
Estimated Value: $200.00 - $250.00

Noble Model 420 EK
A fancy version of the Model 420 with automatic ejectors; select walnut; recoil pad; engraving; gold inlay
Estimated Value: $240.00 - $300.00

Noble Model 450E
Similar to Model 420 EK; made from the late 1960's to the early 1970's
Estimated Value: $275.00 - $350.00

Noble Model 40

Noble Model 50
Same as the Model 40 without recoil pad or "Multi-Choke"
Estimated Value: $105.00 - $130.00

Noble Model 40
Gauge: 12
Action: Slide action; hammerless
Magazine: 5-shot tubular
Barrel: 28" with multi-choke
Finish: Blued; plain walnut pistol grip stock & grooved slide handle; recoil pad
Estimated Value: $120.00 - $150.00

Noble

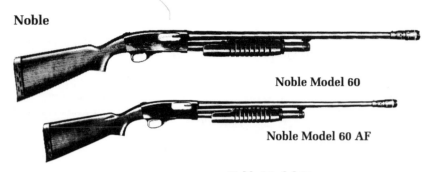

Noble Model 60

Noble Model 60 AF

Noble Model 60 AF
A fancier version of the Model 60
with special steel barrel; select
wood; fluted comb stock
Estimated Value: $125.00 - $160.00

Noble Model 60
Gauge: 12 or 16
Action: Slide action; hammerless
Magazine: 5-shot tubular
Barrel: 28" with variable choke
Finish: Blued; plain walnut pistol
grip stock & grooved slide handle;
recoil pad
Estimated Value: $115.00 - $145.00

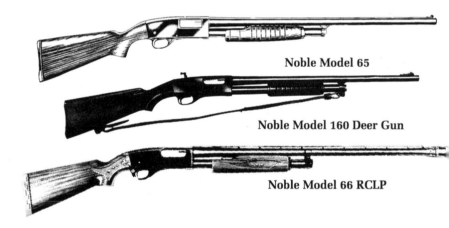

Noble Model 65

Noble Model 160 Deer Gun

Noble Model 66 RCLP

Noble Model 65
Same as the Model 60 except:
without the recoil pad; without
variable choke
Estimated Value: $100.00 - $130.00

**Noble Model 160 Deer Gun, 166L
Deer Gun**
Similar to the Model 60 except: 24"
barrel; sights; swivels; made in the
mid 1960's as model 160; from late
1960's to early 1970's as model 166L
Estimated Value: $130.00 - $165.00

Noble Model 60 ACP
Same as the Model 60 except: it has
ventilated rib
Estimated Value: $125.00 - $160.00

Noble Model 66 RCLP
Similar to the Model 60 ACP with a
fancier checkered stock
Estimated Value: $125.00 - $160.00

Noble Model 70

Noble Model 602

Noble Model 602 CLP

Noble Model 70 & 70X
Gauge: 410
Action: Slide action; hammerless
Magazine: 5-shot tubular
Barrel: 26" modified or full choke
Finish: Blued; checkered walnut pistol grip stock & slide handle; made from the late 1950's to late 1960's as Model 70; late 1960's to early 1970's as 70X
Estimated Value: $130.00 - $165.00

Noble Model 602, CLP, RCLP, RLP
Similar to the Model 70 except: 20 gauge; 28" barrel; grooved slide handle; CLP has adjustable choke; RCLP has recoil pad; RLP has recoil pad & ventilated rib; add 10% for ventilated rib
Estimated Value: $145.00 - $180.00

Noble Model 246

Noble Model 246
Same as Model 249 except: adjustable choke
Estimated Value: $135.00 - $170.00

Noble Model 249
Gauge: 20
Action: Slide action; hammerless
Magazine: 5-shot tubular
Barrel: 28" modified or full choke
Finish: Blued; checkered walnut pistol grip stock & slide handle; recoil pad
Estimated Value: $125.00 - $160.00

Noble Model 243
Same as Model 249 except: it has ventilated rib
Estimated Value: $140.00 - $175.00

Noble

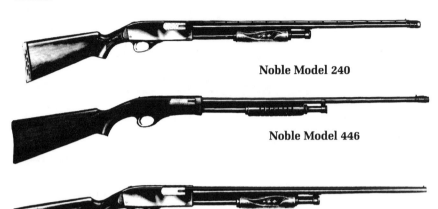

Noble Model 240

Noble Model 446

Noble Model 449

Noble Model 446
Similar to Model 246 except: 410
bore; no recoil pad
Estimated Value: $125.00 - $165.00

Noble Model 240
Same as Model 249 except: it has
adjustable choke & ventilated rib
Estimated Value: $145.00 - $185.00

Noble Model 443
Similar to Model 243 except: 410
bore; no recoil pad
Estimated Value: $130.00 - $170.00

Noble Model 449
Same as the Model 249 except: 410
bore; no recoil pad
Estimated Value: $125.00 - $165.00

Noble Model 440
Similar to Model 240 except: 410
bore; no recoil pad
Estimated Value: $135.00 - $180.00

Noble Model 390 Deer Gun

Noble Model 339
Gauge: 12 or 16
Action: Slide action; hammerless
Magazine: 6-shot tubular
Barrel: 28" modified or full choke
Noble Model 390 Deer Gun
Similar to Model 339 except: 24"
slug barrel; sights; swivels
Estimated Value: $140.00 - $175.00
Finish: Blued; checkered walnut
pistol grip stock & slide handle
Estimated Value: $130.00 - $165.00

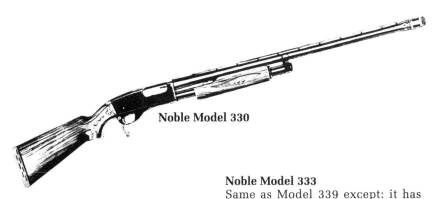

Noble Model 330

Noble Model 333
Same as Model 339 except: it has recoil pad & ventilated rib
Estimated Value: $135.00 - $180.00

Noble Model 330
Same as Model 339 with recoil pad, ventilated rib, & adjustable choke
Estimated Value: $185.00 - $140.00

Noble Model 336
Same as Model 339 except: it has recoil pad & adjustable choke
Estimated Value: $140.00 - $175.00

Noble Model 80

Noble Model 80
Gauge: 410
Action: Semi-automatic; hammerless
Magazine: 5-shot tubular
Barrel: 26" full choke
Finish: Blued; plain walnut pistol grip stock & forearm
Estimated Value: $175.00 - $220.00

Noble Model 757
Gauge: 20
Action: Slide action; hammerless
Magazine: 5-shot tubular
Barrel: 28" aluminum; adjustable choke
Finish: Black anodized aluminum; decorated receiver; checkered walnut pistol grip stock & slide handle; recoil pad
Estimated Value: $130.00 - $175.00

Parker

Parker Trojan
Gauge: 12, 16, or 20
Action: Top lever break-open; hammerless; box lock
Magazine: None
Barrel: Double barrel (side by side); 26", 28", or 30", full & full or modified & full chokes
Finish: Blued; checkered walnut pistol grip stock & forearm
Estimated Value: $1,000.00 - $1,500.00

Parker Single Barrel Trap

Parker Trojan

Parker Hammerless Double
Gauge: 10, 12, 16, 20, 28, or 410
Action: Box lock; top lever, break-open; hammerless; selective trigger & automatic ejectors after 1934
Magazine: None
Barrel: Double barrel (side by side); 26", 28", 30", or 32"; any choke combination
Finish: Blued; checkered walnut straight, full or semi-pistol grip stock & forearm; grades vary according to workmanship, checkering & engraving; manufacture of Parker guns was taken over by Remington in 1934; Priced for pre-1934 models
Estimated Value:
        $1,200.00 - $50,000.00

Parker Single Barrel Trap
Gauge: 12
Action: Slide action; hammerless; top lever break-open; box lock; single shot
Magazine: None; single shot
Barrel: 30", 32", or 34", any choke; ventilated rib
Finish: Blued; checkered walnut straight, full or semi-pistol grip stock; grades differ according to workmanship, checkering, & engraving; manufacture of Parker guns was taken over by Remington in 1934, & this gun was called Remington Parker Model 930; there is a wide range of values for this gun.
Estimated Value:
        $2,000.00 - $12,000.00

Pedersen

Pedersen Model 2500

Pedersen Model 2000 Grade II
Gauge: 12 or 20
Action: Box lock; top lever, break-open; hammerless; automatic ejectors; single selective trigger
Magazine: None
Barrel: Double barrel (side by side); length to customer's specifications
Finish: Blued; checkered walnut pistol grip stock & tapered forearm; engraved
Estimated Value: $1,200.00 - $1,500.00

Pedersen Model 2000 Grade I
Similar to Grade II with fancier engraving, gold filling on receiver, select walnut
Estimated Value: $1,450.00 - $1,800.00

Pedersen Model 2500
A field grade version of the model 2000; no engraving; blade front
Estimated Value: $350.00 - $450.00

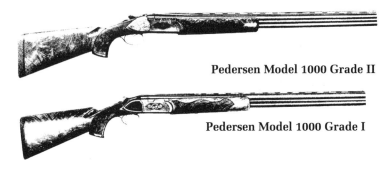

Pedersen Model 1000 Grade II

Pedersen Model 1000 Grade I

Pedersen Model 1000 Grade III
Gauge: 12 or 20
Action: Box lock; top lever, break-open; hammerless; automatic ejectors; single selective trigger
Magazine: None
Barrel: Over & under double barrel; length made to customers specifications; ventilated rib
Finish: Blued; checkered walnut pistol grip stock & forearm; recoil pad
Estimated Value: $600.00 - $800.00

Pedersen Model 1000 Grade II
Similar to Model 1000 Grade III except: engraving & fancier wood; made to customers specs.
Estimated Value: $1,400.00 - $1,725.00

Pedersen Model 1000 Grade I
Similar to Model 1000 Grade II except: extensive engraving, select wood, gold filling on receiver; made to customers specs; hunting, skeet, or trap models
Estimated Value: $1,750.00 - $2,100.00

Pedersen/Premier

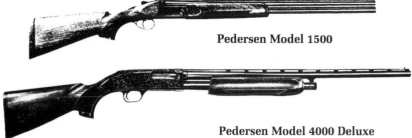

Pedersen Model 1500

Pedersen Model 4000 Deluxe

Pedersen Model 1500
A field version of the Model 1000 Grade III except: standard barrel lengths (26", 28", 30, or 32")
Estimated Value: $400.00 - $500.00

Pedersen Model 4000 Deluxe
Gauge: 10, 12, or 410
Action: Slide action; hammerless; side ejection
Magazine: 5-shot Tubular
Barrel: 26", 28", or 30", variety of chokes; ventilated rib
Finish: Blued; checkered walnut pistol grip stock & slide handle; recoil pad; floral engraving on receiver
Estimated Value: $320.00 - $400.00

Premier

Premier Regent

Premier Brush King

Premier Regent
Gauge: 12, 16, 20, 28, or 410
Action: Box lock; top lever, break-open; hammerless; double triggers
Magazine: None
Barrel: Double barrel (side by side); 26" or 28" modified & full choke; matte rib
Finish: Blued; checkered walnut pistol grip stock & tapered forearm
Estimated Value: $220.00 - $275.00

Premier Brush King
Similar to the Regent except: 12 or 20 gauge only; 22" improved cylinder & modified choke barrels; straight stock
Estimated Value: $225.00 - $285.00

Premier Magnum
Similar to the Regent except: 10 gauge magnum with 32" barrels or 12 gauge magnum with 30" barrels; both gauges in full & full choke; recoil pad; beavertail forearm; add 10% for 20 gauge magnum
Estimated Value: $240.00 - $300.00

Premier Continental

Premier Ambassador
A hammerless version of the Continental. Also available in 410 gauge.
Estimated Value: $350.00 - $280.00

Premier Continental
Gauge: 12, 16, or 20
Action: Side lock; top lever, break-open; exposed hammers; double triggers
Magazine: None
Barrel: Double barrel (side by side); 26" modified & full choke
Finish: Blued; checkered walnut pistol grip stock & tapered forearm
Estimated Value: $260.00 - $325.00

Premier Ambassador

Remington

Remington Model 1893
Gauge: 10, 12, 16, or 20
Action: Top lever, break-open; semi-hammer (cocking lever on left), takedown; single shot
Magazine: None; single shot
Barrel: 28", 30", 32", or 34"; plain barrel
Finish: Blued; case hardened receiver; smooth walnut, pistol grip stock & forearm; also known as the Model No. 3 & the '93
Estimated Value: $155.00 - $195.00

Remington Model 1902 or No. 9
Similar to the Model 1893 except: improved with automatic ejector; made from about 1902 to 1912; also called Model No. 9
Estimated Value: $165.00 - $200.00

Remington Parker 930
Remington took over production of the Parker shotguns from 1934 to 1941; single shot hammerless
Estimated Value: $1,000.00 - $2,500.00

Remington

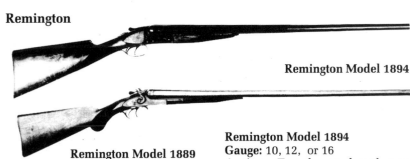

Remington Model 1894

Remington Model 1889

Remington Model 1889
Gauge: 10, 12, or 16
Action: Top lever, break-open; side lock; breech loading black powder; exposed hammers; double trigger
Magazine: None
Barrel: Double barrel (side by side); 28"-32" full, modified or cylinder bores; Damascus or steel barrels
Finish: Blued; checkered walnut semi-pistol grip stock & short forearm; made in seven grades; priced for Standard Grade
Estimated Value: $440.00 - $550.00

Remington Model 1894
Gauge: 10, 12, or 16
Action: Top lever, break-open; concealed hammers; triple lock; double triggers; some models have automatic ejectors
Magazine: None
Barrel: Double barrel (side by side); 26"-32" tapered barrels; full, modified or cylinder bores; ordnance steel or Damascus barrels with concave matted rib
Finish: Blued; checkered walnut, straight or semi-pistol grip stock & short tapered forearm; receivers marked Remington Arms Co. on left side; special engraving & inlays on higher grades; made in seven grades; priced for Standard Grade; deduct $150.00 for Damascus barrels
Estimated Value: $525.00 - $700.00

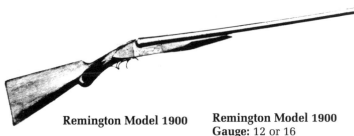

Remington Model 1900

Remington Parker 920
Remington took over production of Parker shotguns from 1934 to 1941; double barrel hammerless; double triggers; 12 gauge
Estimated Value: $750.00 - $1,000.00

Remington Model 1900
Gauge: 12 or 16
Action: Top lever, break-open; concealed hammers; double triggers; automatic ejectors optional
Magazine: None
Barrel: Double barrel (side by side); 28" or 32" steel or Damascus barrels in standard chokes; deduct $100.00 for Damascus barrels; matted rib
Finish: Checkered walnut pistol grip stock & short tapered forearm
Estimated Value: $400.00 - $500.00

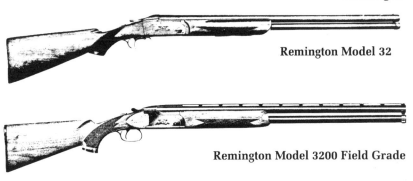

Remington Model 32

Remington Model 3200 Field Grade

Remington Model 32
Gauge: 12
Action: Top lever, break-open; concealed hammers; single selective trigger; automatic ejectors
Magazine: None
Barrel: Over & under double barrel; 26-32" plain; solid or ventilated rib; add 5% for solid rib; add 10% for ventilated rib; full & modified choke standard but any combination available
Finish: Blued; engraved receiver; checkered walnut pistol grip stock & forearm; made in about six grades; priced for standard grade
Estimated Value: $600.00 - $750.00

Remington Model 3200 Field Grade
Gauge: 12
Action: Top lever, break-open; concealed hammers; selective single trigger; automatic ejectors
Magazine: None
Barrel: 26"-30" over & under double barrel; ventilated rib; modified & full or improved cylinder & modified chokes
Finish: Blued; pointing dogs engraved on receiver; checkered walnut pistol grip stock & matching forearm; priced for field grade
Estimated Value: $700.00 - $875.00

Remington Model 3200 Magnum

Remington Model 3200 Special Trap
Similar to the Model 3200 except: 32" barrels; ventilated rib; Monte Carlo stock; recoil pad
Estimated Value: $950.00 - $1,200.00

Remington Model 3200 Magnum
Similar to the Model 3200 Field Grade except: chambered for 12 gauge magnum; 30" barrels in full & full or modified & full chokes; receiver decorated with engraved scrollwork
Estimated Value: $790.00 - $990.00

Remington

Remington Model 3200 Skeet

Remington Model 3200 Competition Trap
Similar to the Model 3200 Special Trap except: higher quality finish
Estimated Value: $975.00 - $1,300.00

Remington Model 3200 Competition Skeet
Similar to the Model 3200 Skeet except: higher quality finish
Estimated Value: $975.00 - $1,300.00

Remington Model 3200 Skeet
Similar to the Model 3200 except: 26" or 28" skeet barrels; ventilated rib ; recoil pad; Monte Carlo stock
Estimated Value: $825.00 - $1,100.00

Remington Model 3200 Pigeon
Similar to the Model 3200 Competition Skeet except: 28" improved modified & full choke barrels for bird hunting
Estimated Value: $1,000.00 - $1,325.00

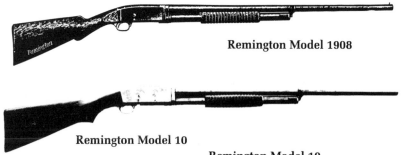

Remington Model 1908

Remington Model 10

Remington Model 1908
Gauge: 12
Action: Slide action; hammerless; bottom ejection; repeating
Magazine: 5-shot tubular
Barrel: 26"-32" steel barrel in full, modified or cylinder bore
Finish: Blued; plain or checkered walnut straight or pistol grip stock & forearm; made in six grades with fancy checkering & engraving on higher grades; priced for field grade
Estimated Value: $250.00 - $325.00

Remington Model 10
Gauge: 12
Action: Slide action; hammerless; bottom ejection; repeating
Magazine: 5-shot tubular
Barrel: 20" barrel riot gun; 26"-32" steel barrel in full, modified or cylinder bore; plain barrel; ventilated or solid rib optional
Finish: Blued; plain or checkered walnut straight or pistol grip stock & forearm; an improved version of the Model 1908; made in seven grades; priced for field grade
Estimated Value: $275.00 - $350.00

Pocket Guide to Shotguns

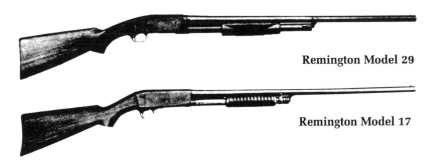

Remington Model 29

Remington Model 17

Remington Model 17
Gauge: 20
Action: Slide action; hammerless; bottom ejection; repeating
Magazine: 3-shot tubular
Barrel: 26"-32" steel in full, modified or cylinder bore; matted sighting groove on receiver or optional solid rib; 20" barrel on riot gun
Finish: Blued; plain or checkered walnut pistol grip stock & forearm; made in seven grades; priced for field grade
Estimated Value: $205.00 - $275.00

Remington Model 29
Gauge: 12
Action: Slide action; hammerless; bottom ejection; repeating
Magazine: 5-shot tubular
Barrel: 26"-32" steel in full, modified or cylinder bore; optional solid or ventilated rib; 20" barrel on riot gun
Finish: Blued; plain or checkered walnut pistol grip stock & forearm; made in nine grades; priced for field grade
Estimated Value: $215.00 - $280.00

Remington Model 31

Remington Model 31 Skeet
Similar to the Model 31 except: 12 gauge only; 26" barrel; solid or ventilated rib; skeet choke; add 8% for ventilated rib
Estimated Value: $360.00 - $450.00

Remington Model 31 R Riot Gun
Similar to the Model 31 except: 12 gauge only; 20" plain barrel
Estimated Value: $170.00 - $225.00

Remington Model 31
Gauge: 12, 16, or 20
Action: Slide action; hammerless; side ejection; repeating
Magazine: 3-shot tubular or 5-shot tubular
Barrel: 26", 32" steel; full, modified, cylinder, or skeet chokes; solid or ventilated rib optional
Finish: Blued; plain or checkered pistol grip stock & forearm; forearm checkered or grooved; made in eight grades; priced for field grade; add 10% for solid rib or ventilated rib
Estimated Value: $220.00 - $275.00

Remington

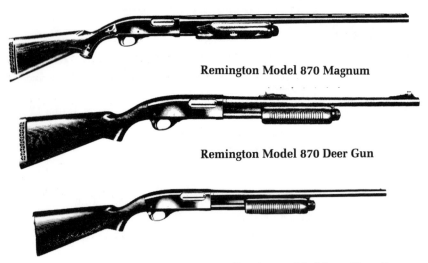

Remington Model 870 Magnum

Remington Model 870 Deer Gun

Remington Model 870 Riot Gun

Remington Model 870 Deer Gun
Similar to the Model 870 AP except:
12 gauge only; 26" barrel for slugs;
rifle type adjustable sights
Estimated Value: $200.00 - $250.00

Remington Model 870 AP
Gauge: 12, 16, or 20
Action: Slide action; hammerless;
side ejection; repeating
Magazine: 4-shot tubular
Barrel: 26" or 28" in 16 & 20 gauge;
30" in 12 gauge; full, modified or
improved cylinder bore; plain or
ventilated rib; add 10% for ventilated rib
Finish: Blued; plain or fancy, fluted
comb, pistol grip stock & grooved
slide handle; made in many grades &
variations; priced for field grade
Estimated Value: $185.00 - $250.00

Remington Model 870 Magnum
Similar to the Model 870 AP except:
12 gauge magnum; 30" full choke
barrel; recoil pad; add 10% for
ventilated rib
Estimated Value: $195.00 - $260.00

Remington Model 870 Riot Gun
Same as the Model 870 AP except:
12 gauge only; 20" plain barrel;
improved cylinder bore
Estimated Value: $180.00 - $225.00

**Remington Model
870 Special Purpose**
Similar to the Model 870 AP except:
oil-finish wood & Parkerized metal;
recoil pad & nylon camo strap; 12
gauge; ventilated rib, 26" or 30"
barrel; "Rem Choke;" deduct 20%
for synthetic stock
Estimated Value: $270.00 - $340.00

Remington Model 870 SP Deer Gun
Similar to the 870 Special Purpose
except: 20" improved cylinder bore
barrel & rifle sights
Estimated Value: $265.00 - $330.00

Pocket Guide to Shotguns

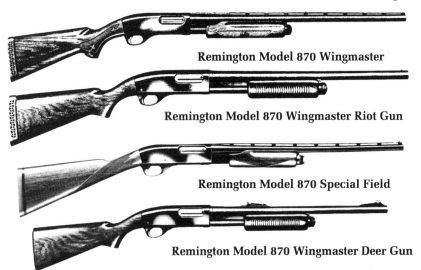

Remington Model 870 Wingmaster

Remington Model 870 Wingmaster Riot Gun

Remington Model 870 Special Field

Remington Model 870 Wingmaster Deer Gun

Remington Model 870
Wingmaster Field Gun
Gauge: 12, 16, or 20; 28 & 410 added in 1969; 16 gauge discontinued in the late 1980's
Action: Slide action; hammerless; side ejection; repeating
Magazine: 4-shot tubular
Barrel: 26"-30" in 12 gauge; 26" or 28" in 16 & 20 gauge; 25" in 28 & 410 bore; add 8% for gauges 28 or 410; full, modified, or improved cylinder bore; plain or ventilated rib barrel
Finish: Blued; checkered walnut pistol grip stock with matching slide handle; recoil pad; lightweight and left hand models optional; add 10% for left hand model; made in many grades; priced for field grade
Estimated Value: $275.00 - $345.00

Remington Model 870 Special Field
Similar to the Model 870 wingmaster except: straight grip stock; 21" ventilated rib barrel; 12 or 20 gauge; 3" chamber; "Rem Choke"optional
Estimated Value: $270.00 - $340.00

Remington Model 870
Wingmaster Magnum
Same as the Model 870 Field Grade except: 12 or 20 gauge magnum only; full or modified choke; add 10% for left hand model; add 10% for "Rem Choke"
Estimated Value: $260.00 - $325.00

Remington Model 870 Wingmaster
Riot Gun, Police
Similar to the Model 870 Wingmaster except: 12 gauge only; 18" or 20" improved cylinder barrel; plain stock & grooved slide handle; designed for law enforcement use; add 8% for rifle sights; blued or parkerized finish
Estimated Value: $205.00 - $260.00

Remington Model 870
Wingmaster Deer Gun
Same as Model 870 Wingmaster except: 12 gauge only; 20" barrel; rifle sights
Estimated Value: $255.00 - $315.00

Remington

Remington Model 870 Brushmaster Deer Gun

Remington Model 870 Ltd. 20
Same as the Model 870 Wingmaster Field except: 20 gauge only; 23" barrel with ventilated rib; lightweight; made from 1980 to 1984
Estimated Value: $310.00 - $250.00

**Remington Model 870
Brushmaster Deer Gun**
Same as the Model 870 Wingmaster Deer Gun except: 12 & 20 gauge; checkered stock & slide; recoil pad; add 8% for 12 gauge
Estimated Value: $250.00 - $310.00

Remington Model 870SA Skeet
Similar to the Model 870 wingmaster except: skeet choke; recoil pad; 25" or 26" ventilated rib barrel
Estimated Value: $240.00 - $300.00

**Remington Model 870
TB Trap, TA Trap, TC Trap**
Similar to the Model 870 wingmaster except: 30" full choke ventilated rib barrel; recoil pad
Estimated Value: $320.00 - $400.00

**Remington Model 870
Competition Trap**
Similar in appearance to the Model 870 except: single shot; 30" full choke ventilated rib barrel; recoil pad; non-glare matte finish receiver
Estimated Value: $425.00 - $570.00

Remington Model 870SP Cantilever
Same as the Model 870SP Deer Gun except: no sights; equipped with cantilever scope mount rings; changeable choke tubes (rifled choke tube for slugs & improved cylinder choke tube)
Estimated Value: $295.00 - $375.00

Remington Model 870 Youth Gun
Same as the Model 870 Wingmaster Field except: 20 gauge only; 21" barrel with ventilated rib; lightweight; short stock; changeable choke tubes after 1985
Estimated Value: $160.00 - $200.00

Pocket Guide to Shotguns

Remington Sportsman 12

Remington Model 870 Express
Gauge: 12 magnum
Action: Slide action; hammerless; side ejection repeating
Magazine: 4-shot tubular
Barrel: 26" or 28" ventilated rib; "Rem Choke"
Finish: Blued; checkered hardwood semi-pistol grip stock & forearm
Estimated Value: $160.00 - $200.00

Remington Sportsman 12 Pump
Gauge: 12; regular or magnum
Action: Slide action; hammerless; side ejection; repeating
Magazine: 4-shot tubular
Barrel: 28" modified, 30" full; ventilated rib; "Rem Choke;" add 10% for "Rem Choke"
Finish: Blued; checkered walnut semi-pistol grip stock & slide handle; steel receiver; recoil pad
Estimated Value: $200.00 - $250.00

Remington Autoloading

Remington Autoloading Riot Gun

Remington Autoloading
Gauge: 12
Action: Semi-automatic; concealed hammer
Magazine: 5-shot tubular
Barrel: 26" or 28" steel; full, modified or cylinder bore
Finish: Blued; matted sight groove; plain or checkered straight or pistol grip stock & forearm; made in six grades; priced for Standard Grade
Estimated Value: $210.00 - $260.00

Remington Autoloading Riot Gun
Similar to the Autoloading Standard Grade except: 20" barrel
Estimated Value: $200.00 - $250.00

Remington

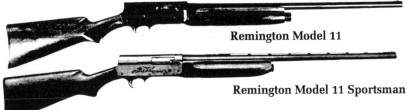

Remington Model 11

Remington Model 11 Sportsman

Remington Model 11 Riot Gun
Same as the Model 11 except; 20"
plain barrel
Estimated Value: $180.00 - $240.00

Remington Model 11 Sportsman
Same as the Model 11 except: 2-shot
magazine; made in six grades; priced
for the Standard Grade; add 10% for
solid or ventilated rib
Estimated Value: $250.00 - $325.00

Remington Model 11
Gauge: 12, 16, or 20
Action: Semi-automatic; concealed
hammer; side ejection; repeating
Magazine: 4-shot tubular
Barrel: 26", 28", 30", or 32"; full,
modified or cylinder choke; solid or
ventilated rib optional; add 10% for
ribbed barrel
Finish: Blued; wood semi-pistol grip
stock; straight grip on Trap grades;
checkering & fancy wood on higher
grades; made in six grades; priced
for Standard Grade
Estimated Value: $200.00 - $260.00

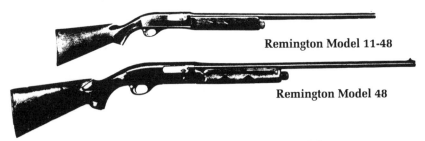

Remington Model 11-48

Remington Model 48

Remington Model 11-48 Riot Gun
Same general specifications as the
Model 11-48 except: 12 gauge only;
20" plain barrel
Estimated Value: $190.00 - $240.00

Remington Model 48
Similar to the Model 11-48 except:
2-shot magazine; 12, 16, or 20 gauge.
Made in several grades; replaced
the Model 11 Sportsman; priced for
Standard Model; add 10% for
ventilated rib
Estimated Value: $180.00 - $225.00

Remington Model 11-48
Gauge: 12, 16, 20, 28, or 410
Action: Semi-auto; hammerless; side
ejection; take down; cross bolt safety
Magazine: 4-shot tubular; 3-shot in
28 & 410 gauges
Barrel: 26", 28", or 30" in 12, 16, & 20
gauge; 25" in 28 & 410 bore; full, modified or improved cylinder choke; add
10% for optional ventilated rib
Finish: Checkered walnut pistol grip
stock with fluted comb, matching
semi-beavertail forearm; higher
grades are fancier; made in about
seven grades; priced for Standard
model
Estimated Value: $215.00 - $265.00

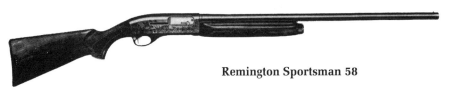

Remington Sportsman 58

Remington Sportsman 58
Gauge: 12, 16, or 20
Action: Semi-automatic; hammerless; side ejection; solid breech; gas operated sliding bolt; fixed barrel
Magazine: 2-shot tubular
Barrel: 26", 28", or 30"; plain or ventilated rib; add 10%for ventilated rib; full, modified, improved cylinder or skeet chokes
Finish: Blued; checkered walnut pistol grip stock with fluted comb & matching semi-beavertail forearm
Estimated Value: $220.00 - $275.00

Remington Sportsman 58 Magnum
Similar to the Sportsman 58 except: 12 gauge magnum; 30" barrel; recoil pad; add 10% for ventilated rib
Estimated Value: $225.00 - $280.00

Remington Sportsman 58 Rifled Slug Special
Same as the Sportsman 58 except: 12 gauge only; 26" barrel for slugs; equipped with rifle sights
Estimated Value: $215.00 - $265.00

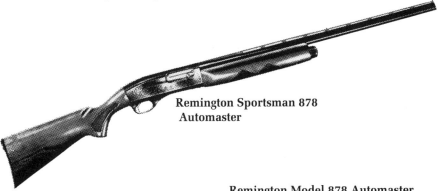

Remington Sportsman 878
Automaster

Remington Sportsman 12 Auto
Gauge: 12
Action: Gas operated semi-automatic
Magazine: 4-shot tubular
Barrel: 28" modified, 30" full; ventilated rib; "Rem Choke"optional; add 10% for "Rem Choke"
Finish: Checkered hardwood semi-pistol grip stock & forearm
Estimated Value: $255.00 - $340.00

Remington Model 878 Automaster
Gauge: 12
Action: Semi-auto; gas operated; hammerless
Magazine: 2-shot tubular
Barrel: 26"-30"; full, modified, improved cylinder or skeet chokes; plain barrel or ventilated rib; add 10% for ventilated rib
Finish: Blued; plain or checkered walnut pistol grip stock & forearm
Estimated Value: $210.00 - $260.00

Remington

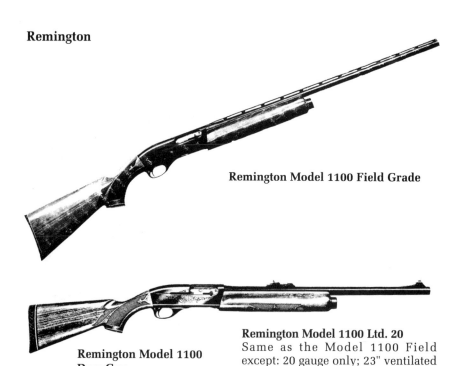

Remington Model 1100 Field Grade

Remington Model 1100 Deer Gun

Remington Model 1100 Field Grade
Gauge: 12, 16, 20, 28, or 410
Action: Semi-auto; gas operated sliding bolt; fixed barrel; solid breech; hammerless; takedown
Magazine: 4-shot tubular
Barrel: 26", 28" in 16 & 20 gauge; 26", 28", 30" in 12 gauge; 25" in 28 & 410; add 8% for gauges 28 or 410; full, modified, improved cylinder & skeet chokes; add 8% for optional "Rem Choke;" add 8% for optional ventilated rib
Finish: Blued; checkered wood pistol grip stock with fluted comb & matching forearm; engraved receiver; made in several grades; add 8% for left hand model
Estimated Value: $350.00 - $440.00

Remington Model 1100 Ltd. 20
Same as the Model 1100 Field except: 20 gauge only; 23" ventilated rib barrel; lightweight
Estimated Value: $320.00 - $400.00

Remington Model 1100 Youth Gun
Same as the Model 1100 Field except: 20 gauge only; 21" ventilated rib barrel; lightweight; short stock; changeable choke tubes after 1985
Estimated Value: $345.00 - $430.00

Remington Model 1100 Magnum
Similar to the Model 1100 Field except: 12 or 20 gauge magnum; 28" or 30" barrel; full or modified chokes; recoil pad; add 8% for left hand model
Estimated Value: $320.00 - $400.00

Remington Model 1100 Deer Gun
Similar to the Model 1100 Field except: 22" plain barrel & adjustable rifle sights; bored for rifled slugs; 12 or 20 gauge lightweight
Estimated Value: $320.00 - $400.00

Remington Model 1100 Special Field

**Remington Model 1100
Special Purpose**
Similar to the Model 1100 Field except: oil-finished wood & Parkerized metal; recoil pad & nylon camo strap; 12 gauge only; ventilated rib barrel
Estimated Value: $345.00 - $460.00

Remington Model 1100 Tournament Skeet
Similar to the Model 1100 SA Skeet with higher quality finish
Estimated Value: $360.00 - $450.00

**Remington Model 1100
SP Deer Gun**
Similar to the Model 1100 Special Purpose except: 21" improved cylinder barrel & rifle sights
Estimated Value: $300.00 - $375.00

Remington Model 1100 SA Skeet
Similar to the Model 1100 Field except: 25" or 26" skeet choke barrel; ventilated rib; scroll receiver; add 8% for left hand model
Estimated Value: $340.00 - $425.00

**Remington Model 1100
Special Field**
Similar to the Model 1100 Field except: straight grip stock & 21" ventilated rib barrel; 12 or 20 gauge
Estimated Value: $350.00 - $440.00

Remington Model 1100 Tournament Trap

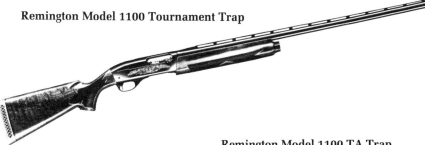

**Remington Model 1100
Tournament Trap**
Similar to the Model 1100 TA Trap with higher quality finish; add $10.00 for Monte Carlo stock
Estimated Value: $425.00 - $565.00

Remington Model 1100 TA Trap
Similar to the Model 1100 Field except: 30" full or modified trap barrel; ventilated rib; recoil pad; add $10.00 for optional Monte Carlo stock; add 8% for left hand model
Estimated Value: $360.00 - $475.00

Remington

Remington Model 11-87 Premier

Remington Model SP-10
Gauge: 10
Action: Gas operated (non-corrosive stainless steel gas system) semi-automatic; safety in rear of trigger guard
Magazine: 3-shot tubular
Barrel: 26" or 30" matte, non-reflective blued finish with ventilated rib; full & modified choke tubes
Finish: Checkered walnut pistol grip stock & forearm with low gloss satin finish to reduce glare
Estimated Value: $560.00 - $700.00

Remington Model 11-87 Premier
Gauge: 12; regular & magnum
Action: Gas operated, semi-automatic
Magazine: 3-shot tubular
Barrel: 26", 28", or 30" with "Rem Choke"
Finish: Blued; checkered walnut pistol grip stock & forearm; add 8% for left hand model
Estimated Value: $365.00 - $455.00

Remington Model 11-87
Premier Skeet
Similar to the Model 11-87 Premier with 26" skeet or "Rem Choke" barrel; add 4% for "Rem Choke"
Estimated Value: $335.00 - $475.00

Remington Model 11-87
Premier Trap
Similar to the Model 11-87 Premier except: 30" barrel; full choke or "Rem Choke;" Monte Carlo or regular stock; add 4% for "Rem Choke" or Monte Carlo stock
Estimated Value: $400.00 - $500.00

Remington Model 11-87
Special Purpose
Similar to the Model 11-87 Premier with a 26" or 30" "Rem Choke" barrel, non-glare finish; recoil pad; ventilated rib; camo strap
Estimated Value: $360.00 - $450.00

Remington Model 11-87 Cantilever
Same as the Model 11-87 Special Purpose Deer Gun except: no sights; equipped with cantilever scope mount, rings & changeable choke tubes (rifled choke tube for slugs & improved cylinder tube)
Estimated Value: $375.00 - $465.00

Remington Model 11-87 Special Purpose Deer Gun
Similar to the Model 11-87 Special Purpose except: 21" improved cylinder barrel & rifle sights
Estimated Value: $350.00 - $435.00

Richland Model 707 Deluxe

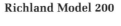

Richland Model 200

Richland Model 200
Gauge: 12, 16, 20, 28, or 410
Action: Box lock; top lever, break-open; hammerless; double trigger
Magazine: None
Barrel: Double barrel (side by side); 22" improved cylinder & modified in 20 gauge; 26" or 28" improved & modified or modified & full chokes
Finish: Blued; checkered walnut pistol grip stock & tapered forearm; cheekpiece; recoil pad
Estimated Value: $220.00 - $275.00

Richland Model 707 Deluxe
Gauge: 12 or 20
Action: Box lock; top lever, break-open; hammerless; double trigger
Magazine: None
Barrel: Double barrel (side by side); 26", 28", or 30"; variety of chokes
Finish: Blued; checkered walnut pistol grip stock & tapered forearm; recoil pad
Estimated Value: $250.00 - $310.00

Richland Model 202
Same as the Model 200 except: extra set of barrels
Estimated Value: $290.00 - $375.00

Richland Model 711 Long Range Waterfowl

Richland Model 747
Gauge: 12 or 20, magnum
Action: Box lock; top lever, break-open; hammerless; single selective trigger
Magazine: None
Barrel: Over & under double barrel; 22" or 26" improved cylinder & modified, 28" modified & full
Finish: Blued; gray receiver; checkered walnut pistol grip stock & forearm; ventilated rib
Estimated Value: $255.00 - $340.00

Richland Model 711 Long Range Waterfowl
Gauge: 10 or 12; magnum
Action: Box lock; top lever, break-open; hammerless; double trigger
Magazine: None
Barrel: Double barrel (side by side); 30" or 32" full choke
Finish: Blued; checkered walnut pistol grip stock & tapered forearm
Estimated Value: $220.00 - $295.00

Richland

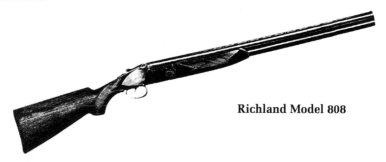

Richland Model 808

Richland Model 808
Gauge: 12
Action: Box lock; top lever, break-open; hammerless; non-selective single trigger
Magazine: None
Barrel: Over & under double barrel; 26" improved cylinder & modified; 28" modified & full; 30" full & full; ventilated rib
Finish: Blued; checkered walnut pistol grip stock & forearm
Estimated Value: $300.00 - $375.00

Richland Model 844
Gauge: 12; magnum
Action: Box lock; top lever, break-open; hammerless; non-selective single trigger
Magazine: None
Barrel: Over & under double barrel; 26" improved cylinder & modified; 28" modified & full; 30" full & full; ventilated rib
Finish: Blued; checkered walnut pistol grip stock & forearm
Estimated Value: $320.00 - $390.00

Richland Model 828

Richland Model 828
Gauge: 28
Action: Box lock; top lever, break-open; hammerless
Magazine: None
Barrel: Over & under double barrel; 26" improved & modified; 28" modified & full chokes; ventilated rib
Finish: Blued; case hardened receiver; checkered walnut pistol grip stock & forearm
Estimated Value: $275.00 - $350.00

Richland Model 41 Ultra
Gauge: 410
Action: Box lock; top lever, break-open; hammerless; single non-selective trigger
Magazine: None
Barrel: Over & under double barrel; 26" chrome lined, modified & full; ventilated rib
Finish: Blued; gray engraved receiver; checkered walnut pistol grip stock & forearm
Estimated Value: $200.00 - $275.00

Pocket Guide to Shotguns

Ruger

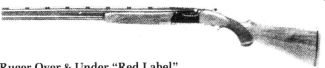

Ruger Over & Under "Red Label"

Ruger "Red Label" Sporting Clay
Similar to Ruger Over & Under Red Label except: 12 gauge only (3" chambers); 30" barrels; checkered walnut pistol grip stock and forearm; four screw-in chokes with each gun (modified, improved cylinder, and two skeet chokes)
Estimated Value: $775.00 - $965.00

Ruger Over & Under "Red Label"
Gauge: 12 or 20 (3" chambers)
Action: Box lock; top lever, break-open; hammerless; single selective trigger
Magazine: None
Barrel: Over & under double barrel; 26" or 28" with a variety of screw-in chokes; ventilated rib;
Finish: Blued; stainless steel receiver on 12 gauge after 1985 and on 20 gauge after 1989; checkered walnut, straight or pistol grip stock & semi-beavertail forearm; recoil pad
Estimated Value: $690.00 - $865.00

SKB

SKB 500

SKB Model 500, 505F & 505CF
Gauge: 12 magnum, 20, 28, or 410
Action: Box lock; top lever, break-open; hammerless
Magazine: None
Barrel: Over & under double barrel; 26" improved cylinder & modified; 28" or 30" modified & full; ventilated rib; chrome lined; 505CF has "inter" choke system
Finish: Blued; checkered walnut pistol grip stock & forearm; recoil pad on magnum; engraved receiver on Model 500; Made from the mid-1960's to mid-1980's as Model 500; to present as model 505
Estimated Value: $700.00 - $875.00

SKB Model 505 Trap
Similar to the Model 505 except: 12 gauge only, 30" or 32" "Inter Choke" barrels
Estimated Value: $710.00 - $885.00

SKB

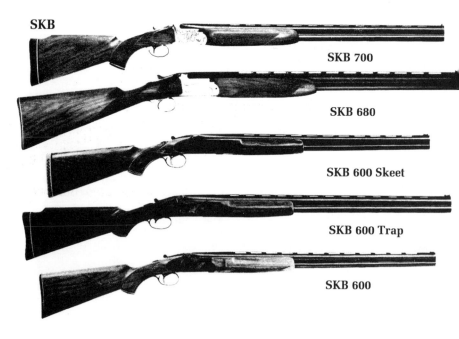

SKB 700

SKB 680

SKB 600 Skeet

SKB 600 Trap

SKB 600

SKB Model 885
Similar to the Model 505 except: engraved silver-plated receiver sideplates; add 3% for Trap or Skeet Model
Estimated Value: $870.00 - $1,085.00

SKB Model 500 Skeet & 505 CSK
Similar to the Model 500 except: 26" or 28" skeet choke barrels; Model 500 discontinued in mid-1980's & replaced by Model 505CSK
Estimated Value: $730.00 - $915.00

SKB Model 600 Trap & 605 Trap
Similar to the 600 except: regular or Monte Carlo stock; 12 gauge only; recoil pad, 30" or 32" full choke barrels on Model 600; "inter" choke system available on Model 605 Trap (late 1980's)
Estimated Value: $950.00 - $1,195.00

SKB Model 600 & 605F
Similar to the 500 except: select wood; trigger mounted barrel selector; silver-plate receiver
Estimated Value: $585.00 - $730.00

SKB Model 600 Skeet & 605 CSK
Similar to the 600 except: 26" or 28" skeet choke barrels (Model 600) & recoil pad; "inter" choke system on 605CSK (late 1980's)
Estimated Value: $950.00 - $1,195.00

SKB Model 680
Similar to the 600 except: a straight grip stock
Estimated Value: $640.00 - $800.00

SKB Model 700
Similar to the 600 except: higher quality finish & more extensive engraving
Estimated Value: $680.00 - $850.00

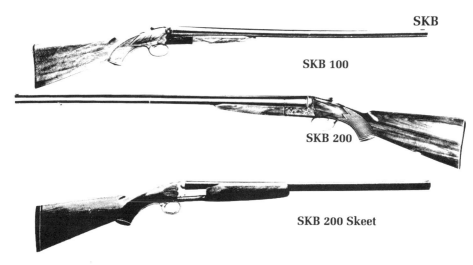

SKB 100

SKB 200

SKB 200 Skeet

SKB Model 100
Gauge: 12 or 20; magnum
Action: Box lock; top lever, break-open; hammerless; single selective trigger
Magazine: None
Barrel: Double barrel (side by side); 26" or 28" improved cylinder & modified or 30" full & full choke in 12 gauge
Finish: Blued; checkered hardwood pistol grip stock & short tapered forearm
Estimated Value: $225.00 - $300.00

SKB Model 200 Skeet
Similar to the 200 except: 25" skeet choke barrels & recoil pad
Estimated Value: $420.00 - $525.00

SKB Model 200 & 200E
Similar to the Model 100 except: engraved silver-plate receiver; wide forearm; select walnut; automatic selective ejectors; 200E has straight grip stock
Estimated Value: $530.00 - $670.00

SKB 280

SKB Model 400
Similar to the Model 200 & 200E except: sideplate receiver
Estimated Value: $715.00 - $895.00

SKB Model 280
Similar to the 200 except: without silver-plate receiver; straight grip stock
Estimated Value: $375.00 - $500.00

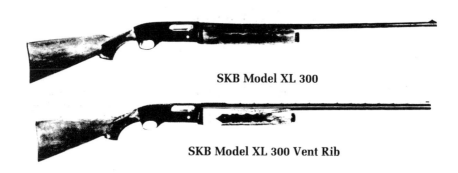

SKB Model XL 300

SKB Model XL 300 Vent Rib

SKB Model 1300
Gauge: 12 or 20; regular or magnum
Action: Semi-automatic
Magazine: 5-shot tubular
Barrel: 26" or 28" "Inter Choke;"
ventilated rib; slug barrel with rifle
sights optional
Finish: Blued, black receiver;
checkered walnut pistol grip stock &
forearm
Estimated Value: $430.00 - $540.00

SKB Model 1900
Similar to the Model 1300 except:
light-weight receiver featuring
engraved hunting scene; gold-plated
trigger; add 5% for 30" barrel Trap
Model
Estimated Value: $330.00 - $410.00

SKB Model 3000
A presentation deluxe version of the
Model 1900; Highback receiver; add
2% for optional trap version
Estimated Value: $350.00 - $435.00

SKB Model XL 300
Gauge: 12 or 20
Action: Gas operated; semi-
automatic; hammerless
Magazine: 5-shot tubular
Barrel: 26" improved cylinder or
skeet; 28" modified or full; 30"
modified or full chokes
Finish: Blued; decorated receiver;
checkered walnut pistol grip stock &
forearm
Estimated Value: $220.00 - $275.00

SKB XL 300 Vent Rib
Similar to the XL 300 except:
ventilated rib
Estimated Value: $240.00 - $300.00

SKB Model XL 100 Slug
Similar to the Model XL 300; a no-
frills slug gun with 20" barrel; rifle
sights; swivels
Estimated Value: $175.00 - $235.00

SKB Model XL 900

SKB Model XL 900 Slug
Similar to the XL 900 except: 24"
barrel for slugs; rifle sights; swivels
Estimated Value: $230.00 - $310.00

SKB Model XL 900
Similar to the XL 300 except:
Ventilated rib with engraved silver-
plated receiver; gold-plated trigger
Estimated Value: $260.00 - $325.00

SKB Model XL 900 Skeet
Similar to the XL 900 Trap except:
skeet stock & skeet choke barrel
Estimated Value: $250.00 - $330.00

SKB Model XL 900 Trap
Similar to the XL 900 except:
without silver-plated receiver; recoil
pad; choice of regular or Monte
Carlo stock
Estimated Value: $280.00 - $350.00

SKB Model XL 900 MR
Similar to the XL 900 except: 3"
magnum shells; recoil pad; deduct
10% for slug model
Estimated Value: $260.00 - $350.00

Sarasqueta

Sarasqueta Sidelock Grades 4 to 12
Gauge: 12, 16, 20, or 28
Action: Side lock; top lever, break-
open; hammerless; double triggers
Magazine: None
Barrel: Double barrel (side by side);
standard barrel lengths & chokes to
customer's specifications
Finish: Blued; checkered walnut
straight or pistol grip stock &
forearm; grades differ as to quality &
extent of engraving
Estimated Value: $550.00 - $2,500.00

Sarasqueta Sidelock

Sarasqueta/Sauer

Sarasqueta Over & Under Deluxe
Gauge: 12
Action: Side lock; top lever, break-open; hammerless; double triggers; automatic ejectors
Magazine: None
Barrel: Over & under double barrel; lengths & chokes made to customer's specifications
Finish: Blued; checkered walnut pistol grip stock & forearm
Estimated Value: $850.00 - $1,200.00

Sarasqueta Model 2 & 3
Gauge: 12, 16, 20, or 28
Action: Box lock; top lever, break-open; hammerless; double triggers
Magazine: None
Barrel: Double barrel (side by side); standard barrel lengths & chokes; as per customer's specifications
Finish: Blued; checkered walnut straight grip stock & forearm; grades differ only in engraving style
Estimated Value: $325.00 - $550.00

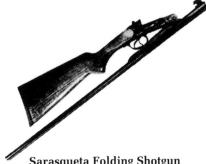

Sarasqueta Folding Shotgun
Gauge: 410
Action: Box lock; top lever, break-open; exposed hammer
Magazine: None
Barrel: Double barrel (side by side); 26" choice of chokes
Finish: Blued; case-hardened receiver; walnut pistol grip stock & forearm
Estimated Value: $115.00 - $150.00

Sarasqueta Folding Shotgun

Sauer

Sauer Royal

Sauer Royal
Gauge: 12 or 20
Action: Box lock; top lever, break-open; hammerless; automatic ejectors; single selective trigger
Magazine: None
Barrel: Double barrel (side by side); 28" modified & full, 26" improved & modified in 20 gauge; 30" full in 12 gauge
Finish: Blued; engraved receiver; checkered walnut pistol grip stock & tapered forearm; recoil pad
Estimated Value: $890.00 - $1,100.00

Sauer Model 66 Field Grade

Sauer Model 66 Trap Grade

Sauer Model BBF

Sauer Model 66 Field Grade
Gauge: 12
Action: Purdey action; hammerless; single selective trigger; automatic ejectors
Magazine: None
Barrel: Over & under double barrel; 28" modified & full choke; ventilated rib
Finish: Blued; checkered walnut pistol grip stock & forearm; recoil pad; engraving. Priced for Field grade. Grades II & III differ in quality & extent of engraving
Estimated Value: $1,200.00 - $1,500.00

Sauer Model 66 Skeet
Basically the same as the Trap Model except: 25" barrels in skeet choke
Estimated Value: $1,220.00 - $1,525.00

Sauer Model 66 Trap Grade
Basically the same as the Field Grade except: 30" barrels & a trap stock; produced in three grades
Estimated Value: $1,240.00 - $1,550.00

Sauer Model BBF
Gauge: 16
Caliber: 30-30, 30-06, or 7 x 65
Action: Kersten lock; Blitz action; top lever, break-open; hammerless; double trigger
Magazine: None
Barrel: Over & under rifle-shotgun combination; 25" Krupp barrels; rifle barrel & full choke shotgun barrel
Finish: Blued; checkered walnut Monte Carlo pistol grip stock & forearm; engraved; sights; swivels; also available in deluxe model with extensive engraving
Estimated Value: $1,200.00 - $1,600.00

Savage

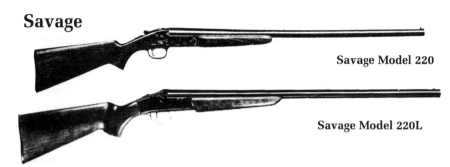

Savage Model 220

Savage Model 220L

Savage Model 220P
Basically the same as 220 except: no 410 gauge; "Poly-Choke" & recoil pad
Estimated Value: $80.00 - $100.00

Savage Model 220L
Similar to Model 220 except: side lever, break-open
Estimated Value: $65.00 - $85.00

Savage Model 220
Gauge: 12, 16, 20, 28, or 410
Action: Top lever, break-open; single shot; hammerless; automatic ejector
Magazine: None
Barrel: Full choke; 28", 30", 32" in 12 & 16 gauge; 26", 28", 30", 32" in 20 gauge; 28" & 30" in 28 gauge; 26" & 28" in 410 bore
Finish: Blued; plain wood, pistol grip stock & forearm
Comments: Made from 1930's until late 1940's; reintroduced in the mid-1950's with 36" barrel; replaced by 220L in mid-1960's
Estimated Value: $70.00 - $90.00

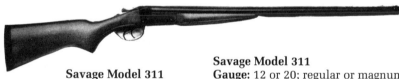

Savage Model 311

Savage Model 311
Gauge: 12 or 20; regular or magnum
Action: Top lever, break-open; hammerless, double trigger
Magazine: None
Barrel: Double barrel (side by side); 28" modified & full; matted rib
Finish: Blued; hardwood, semi-pistol grip stock & tapered forearm; the Model 311 was originally a Stevens shotgun; in 1988 Savage dropped the Stevens designation.
Estimated Value: $185.00 - $230.00

Savage Model 311 Waterfowler
Similar to the Model 311 with Parkerized finish
Estimated Value: $185.00 - $230.00

Savage Model 242

Savage Model 24F Combination
Gauge: 20 or 12; 3" chamber
Caliber: 22 long rifle, 22 Hornet, 222 Rem., 223 Rem., 30-30 Win.
Action: Top lever, break open; exposed hammer with barrel selector; hammer block safety
Magazine: None
Barrel: 24" rifle barrel over 24" shotgun barrel; any combination of rifle caliber & shotgun gauge; shotgun barrel in modified choke; modified & full choke tubes optional; add 4% for choke tubes
Finish: DuPont Rynite® two-piece stock & forearm
Estimated Value: $225.00 - $245.00

Savage Model 24V Combination
Same as the Model 24F Combination except: walnut finish hardwood stock & forearm; 20 gauge, 3" chamber under 222 Rem., 223 Rem., or 30-30 Win. rifle barrel
Estimated Value: $200.00 - $250.00

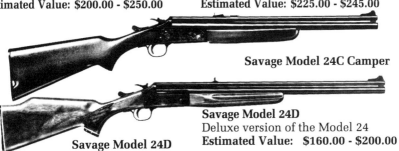

Savage Model 24C Camper

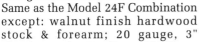

Savage Model 24D

Savage Model 24D
Deluxe version of the Model 24
Estimated Value: $160.00 - $200.00

Savage Model 24
Gauge: 20 or 410
Caliber: 22 short, long, long rifle; 22 magnum
Action: Top lever, break open; exposed hammer; single trigger with barrel slector
Magazine: None
Barrel: Over & under double barrel; 24" rifle barrel over shotgun barrel
Finish: Blued; checkered walnut finish hardwood pistol grip stock & forearm; sporting rear & ramp front sights; case hardened receiver
Estimated Value: $145.00 - $180.00

Savage Model 24C Camper, 24CS
A shorter version of the Model 24 with a 20" barrel; 22LR over 20 gauge barrel; buttplate opens for ammo storage; add $45.00 for satin nickel finish (24CS) & extra pistol grip stock
Estimated Value: $150.00 - $190.00

Savage Model 242
Similar to the Model 24 with 410 gauge over & under shotgun barrels; full choke; bead sights
Estimated Value: $130.00 - $160.00

Savage

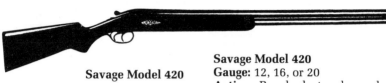

Savage Model 420

Savage Model 389
Gauge: 12; regular or magnum
Caliber: 222 or 308
Action: Top lever, break-open; hammerless; double trigger; shotgun barrel over rifle barrel; tang safety
Magazine: None
Barrel: 25¾" over & under double barrel; changeable choke tubes
Finish: Blued; checkered walnut pistol grip stock & forearm; sling studs
Estimated Value: $550.00 - $670.00

Savage Model 420
Gauge: 12, 16, or 20
Action: Box lock; top lever, break-open; hammerless; double triggers or non-selective single trigger; add $25.00 for single trigger
Magazine: None
Barrel: Over & under double barrel; 26" - 30" modified & full or cylinder bore & modified chokes
Finish: Blued; plain walnut pistol grip stock & forearm
Estimated Value: $320.00 - $400.00

Savage Model 430
Similar as Model 420 except: special checkered walnut stock & forearm; matted upper barrel; recoil pad; add $25.00 for single trigger
Estimated Value: $360.00 - $450.00

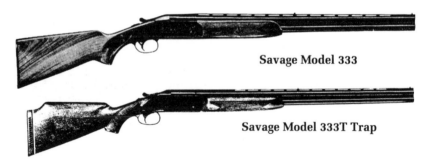

Savage Model 333

Savage Model 333T Trap

Savage Model 333
Gauge: 12 or 20
Action: Top lever, break-open; hammerless; single trigger
Magazine: None
Barrel: Over & under double barrel; 26" - 30"; variety of chokes; ventilated rib
Finish: Blued; checkered walnut pistol grip stock & forearm
Estimated Value: $375.00 - $500.00

Savage Model 333T Trap
Similar to 333 except: Monte Carlo stock; recoil pad; 12 gauge; 30" barrel
Estimated Value: $395.00 - $525.00

Savage Model 330
Similar to 333 except: no ventilated rib
Estimated Value: $340.00 - $450.00

Savage Model 312 Field
Gauge: 12; regular or magnum
Action: Top lever, break-open; concealed hammers; single trigger with safety acting as barrel selector
Magazine: None
Barrel: Over & under double barrel; 26" or 28"; ventilated rib; changeable choke tubes in full, modified, & improved cylinder
Finish: Blued; satin chrome receiver; cut-checkered walnut pistol grip stock & matching forearm; recoil pad
Estimated Value: $325.00 - $405.00

Savage Model 320 Field
Same as the Savage Model 312 Field except: 20 gauge (3" chambers) with 26" barrels
Estimated Value: $325.00 - $405.00

Savage Model 312T
Same as Model 312 Field except: 30" barrels; two full & one modified choke tubes; Monte Carlo stock
Estimated Value: $345.00 - $430.00

Savage Model 312 SC
Same as the Model 312 Field except: 28" barrels only; seven choke tubes included (one full, two improved cylinder, two modified, one #1 skeet & one #2 skeet); "Sporting Clays" engraved on receiver
Estimated Value: $330.00 - $415.00

Savage Model 28A

Savage Model 28D Trap

Savage Model 28C Riot
Basically the same as model 28A except: 20" cylinder bore barrel; used by police, bank guards, etc. for protection
Estimated Value: $150.00 - $190.00

Savage Model 28A & B Standard
Gauge: 12
Action: Slide action; hammerless; solid breech; side ejection
Magazine: 5-shot tubular
Barrel: 26", 28", 30", or 32" cylinder, modified or full choke; matted rib on 28B; add $10.00 for matted rib
Finish: Blued; checkered wood pistol grip stock & grooved slide handle
Estimated Value: $175.00 - $220.00

Savage Model 28D Trap
Same as model 28B except: special straight grip checkered walnut stock and slide handle; 30" full choke barrel
Estimated Value: $190.00 - $240.00

Savage Model 28S Special
Same as model 28B except: ivory bead front sight; checkered pistol grip stock and forearm
Estimated Value: $180.00 - $225.00

Savage

Savage Model 30

Savage Model 30 FG

Savage Model 30 AC

Savage Model 30D

Savage Model 30 FG Slug Gun
Same as Model 30 FG except: 22"
barrel; rifle sights; 12 gauge
Estimated Value: $140.00 - $175.00

Savage Model 30
Gauge: 12, 20, or 410
Action: Slide action; hammerless
Magazine: 4-shot tubular
Barrel: 26", 28", or 30"; cylinder
bore, modified or full choke;
ventilated rib
Finish: Blued; decorated receiver;
walnut pistol grip stock & grooved
slide handle
Estimated Value: $160.00 - $200.00

Savage Model 30 FG (Field Grade)
Similar to Model 30 except: plain
receiver; no ventilated rib
Estimated Value: $130.00 - $160.00

Savage Model 30 AC
Same as Model 30 FG except:
adjustable choke
Estimated Value: $135.00 - $170.00

Savage Model 30D (Deluxe)
1970's version of the Model 30 with
recoil pad grooved slide handle
Estimated Value: $130.00 - $175.00

Savage Model 30T Trap
Fancy version of Model 30 in 12
gauge; 30" full choke barrel; Monte
Carlo stock; recoil pad
Estimated Value: $165.00 - $210.00

Pocket Guide to Shotguns

Savage Model 69 RXL

Savage Model 67
Gauge: 12 or 20; regular or magnum
Action: Slide action; hammerless; side ejecting; repeating
Magazine: 4-shot tubular, 3-shot in magnum
Barrel: 28"; modified
Finish: Blued; hardwood, semi-pistol grip stock & grooved slide handle; the Model 67 was originally a Stevens shotgun; in 1988 Savage dropped the Stevens designation.
Estimated Value: $145.00 - $180.00

Savage Model 67 VRT
Similar to the Model 67 except: ventilated rib; interchangeable choke tubes; recoil pad
Estimated Value: $170.00 - $210.00

Savage Model 67 Slug
Similar to Model 67 except: 21" cylinder bore barrel; recoil pad; rifle sights & scope mount
Estimated Value: $150.00 - $195.00

Savage Model 69R, 69N, 69RXL, 69RXG
Gauge: 12; regular or magnum
Action: Slide action; hammerless
Magazine: 6-shot tubular, 4-shot in 69R
Barrel: 18¼" cylinder bore; 20" on 69R
Finish: Blued; walnut stock & grooved slide handle; recoil pad, swivels; 69N has satin nickel finish; add 30% for satin nickel finish; 69RXG has plastic pistol grip & sling; a law enforcement gun introduced in 1982.
Estimated Value: $145.00 - $190.00

Savage Model 720

Savage Model 720 P
Same as Model 720 except: a "Poly-Choke"
Estimated Value: $215.00 - $270.00

Savage Model 720
Gauge: 12
Action: Browning patent; semi-automatic; hammerless
Magazine: 4-shot tubular
Barrel: 28", 30", or 32" cylinder bore, modified or full choke; in the early 1940's Model 720R (Riot Gun) was introduced with a 20" barrel.
Finish: Blued; checkered walnut pistol grip stock & forearm; engraved receiver, after 1940
Estimated Value: $210.00 - $265.00

Savage

Savage Model 723

Savage Model 726 Upland Sporter

Savage Model 721
Same as Model 720 except: matted rib
Estimated Value: $220.00 - $275.00

Savage Model 723
Same as Model 720 except: 28" or 30" barrel; 12 or 16 gauge
Estimated Value: $205.00 - $260.00

Savage Model 722
Same as Model 720 except: ventilated rib
Estimated Value: $230.00 - $290.00

Savage Model 724
Same as Model 723 except: matted rib
Estimated Value: $220.00 - $275.00

Savage Model 725
Same as Model 723 except: ventilated rib
Estimated Value: $230.00 - $290.00

Savage Model 726 Upland Sporter
Basically the same as Model 720 except: 28" or 30" barrel; 2-shot tubular magazine; 12 or 16 gauge; decorated receiver
Estimated Value: $220.00 - $275.00

Savage Model 727 Upland Sporter
Same as Model 726 Upland Sporter except: matted rib
Estimated Value: $230.00 - $285.00

Savage Model 728 Upland Sporter
Same as Model 726 Upland Sporter except: ventilated rib
Estimated Value: $240.00 - $300.00

Savage Model 740C Skeet Gun
Basically the same as Model 726 Upland Sporter except: skeet stock & "Cutts Compensator"
Estimated Value: $225.00 - $280.00

Savage Model 745 Lightweight
Similar to Model 720 except: light alloy receiver
Estimated Value: $210.00 - $260.00

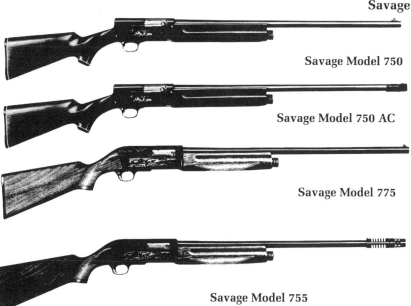

Savage

Savage Model 750

Savage Model 750 AC

Savage Model 775

Savage Model 775 - SC

Savage Model 750
Gauge: 12
Action: Browning patent; semi-automatic; hammerless
Magazine: 4-shot tubular
Barrel: 26" cylinder bore; 28" full or modified
Finish: Blued; checkered walnut pistol grip stock & forearm; decorated receiver
Estimated Value: $240.00 - $300.00

Savage Model 750 SC
Same as Model 750 except: Savage "Super Choke"
Estimated Value: $250.00 - $310.00

Savage Model 750 AC
Same as Model 750 except: adjustable choke
Estimated Value: $220.00 - $275.00

Savage Model 755
Gauge: 12 or 16
Action: Semi-automatic; hammerless
Magazine: 4-shot tubular; 3-shot tubular
Barrel: 26" cylinder bore; 28" full or modified; 30" full choke
Finish: Blued; checkered walnut pistol grip stock & forearm
Estimated Value: $195.00 - $240.00

Savage Model 755 - SC
Same as Model 755 except: Savage "Super Choke"
Estimated Value: $200.00 - $250.00

Savage Model 775 Lightweight
Same as Model 755 except: alloy receiver
Estimated Value: $190.00 - $235.00

Savage Model 775 - SC
Basically the same as Model 775 Lightweight except: Savage "Super Choke;" 26" barrel
Estimated Value: $200.00 - $245.00

Sears

Sears Single Barrel

Sears Double Barrel

Sears Single Barrel
Gauge: 12, 20, or 410
Action: Box lock; top lever, break-open; exposed hammer; automatic ejector
Magazine: None
Barrel: 26" in 410 ga.; 28" in 20 ga.; 30" in 12 ga.; full choke
Finish: Blued; wood pistol grip stock & forearm
Estimated Value: $65.00 - $80.00

Sears Double Barrel
Gauge: 12 or 20
Action: Box lock; top lever, break-open; hammerless; double triggers
Magazine: None
Barrel: Double barrel (side by side); 28"; variety of chokes
Finish: Blued; epoxied black frame; walnut pistol grip stock & forearm
Estimated Value: $160.00 - $200.00

Sears Ted Williams Over & Under

Sears Ted Williams Over & Under
Gauge: 12 or 20
Action: Box lock; top lever, break-open; hammerless; automatic ejectors, selective trigger
Magazine: None
Barrel: Over & under double barrel; 26" or 28" in standard chokes; ventilated rib; chrome lined barrel
Finish: Blued; engraved steel receiver; checkered walnut pistol grip stock & forearm; recoil pad
Estimated Value: $320.00 - $400.00

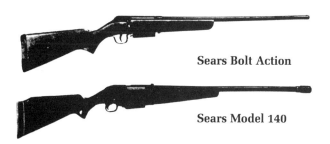

Sears Bolt Action

Sears Model 140

Sears Bolt Action
Gauge: 410
Action: Bolt action; repeating
Magazine: 3-shot detachable clip
Barrel: 24"; full choke
Finish: Blued; wood pistol grip stock & forearm
Estimated Value: $75.00 - $95.00

Sears Model 140
Gauge: 12 or 20
Action: Bolt action; repeating
Magazine: 2-shot detachable clip
Barrel: 25"; adjustable choke
Finish: Blued; wood pistol grip stock & forearm
Estimated Value: $70.00 - $90.00

Sears Model 200

Sears Ted Williams 200

Sears Model 200
Gauge: 12 or 20
Action: Slide action; hammerless; repeating
Magazine: 4-shot tubular
Barrel: 28"; full or modified choke; add 10% for variable choke
Finish: Blued; alloy receiver; wood pistol grip stock & forearm; recoil pad
Estimated Value: $140.00 - $175.00

Sears Ted Williams 300
Gauge: 12 or 20
Action: Semi-auto, gas operated; hammerless
Magazine: 3-shot tubular
Barrel: 28" modified or full choke; 27" adjustable choke; add 5% for variable choke; ventilated rib
Finish: Blued; checkered walnut pistol grip stock & forearm; recoil pad
Estimated Value: $200.00 - $250.00

Sears Ted Williams 200
A fancier version of the Model 200 with checkered wood
Estimated Value: $160.00 - $200.00

Pocket Guide to Shotguns

Smith & Wesson

Smith & Wesson Model 916

Smith & Wesson Model 1000

Smith & Wesson Model 916
Gauge: 12
Action: Slide action; hammerless; side ejection
Magazine: 5-shot tubular
Barrel: Add 10% for 20" cylinder bore; 26" improved cylinder, 28" modified, full or cylinder bore; add 10% for optional ventilated rib
Finish: Blued; satin finish receiver; walnut semi-pistol grip stock & grooved slide handle; recoil pad
Estimated Value: $140.00 - $175.00

Smith & Wesson Model 1000
Gauge: 12 or 20; regular or magnum; add 10% for magnum
Action: Semi-automatic, gas operated; hammerless; side ejection
Magazine: 3-shot tubular
Barrel: 26", 28", or 30"; variety of chokes; add 10% for "Multi-Choke" system; ventilated rib
Finish: Blued; engraved alloy receiver; steel receiver on magnum; checkered walnut pistol grip stock & forearm; sights
Estimated Value: $285.00 - $380.00

Smith & Wesson Model 1000 Super 12
Similar to the Model 1000 except: "Multi-Choke" system; designed to use magnum shells
Estimated Value: $335.00 - $450.00

Smith & Wesson Model 1000 Trap
Similar to the Model 1000 except: Monte Carlo stock; steel receiver; 30" multi-choke barrel; other trap features
Estimated Value: $340.00 - $450.00

Smith & Wesson Model 1000 Slug
Similar to the Model 1000 except: 22" slug barrel; rifle sights & steel receiver
Estimated Value: $285.00 - $380.00

Smith & Wesson Model 1000S, Superskeet
Similar to the Model 1000 except: 25" skeet choke barrel; muzzle vents & other extras; add 50% for Superskeet Model
Estimated Value: $320.00 - $400.00

Pocket Guide to Shotguns

Smith & Wesson Model 1000 Waterfowler

Similar to the Model 1000 except: steel receiver; dull oil-finish stock; 30" full choke barrel; Parkerized finish; swivels; recoil pad; camouflage sling
Estimated Value: $325.00 - $435.00

Smith & Wesson Model 1000 Super 12 Waterfowler

Similar to the Model 1000 Waterfowler except: "Multi-Choke" system
Estimated Value: $350.00 - $470.00

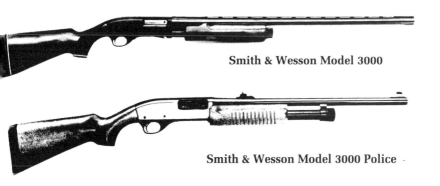

Smith & Wesson Model 3000

Smith & Wesson Model 3000 Police

Smith & Wesson Model 3000

Gauge: 12 or 20; regular or magnum
Action: Slide action; repeating; hammerless
Magazine: 3-shot tubular
Barrel: 26" improved cylinder; 28" modified or full; 30" full; add 10% for "Multi-Choke" system; ventilated rib
Finish: Blued; checkered walnut pistol grip stock & fluted slide handle; recoil pad
Estimated Value: $225.00 - $300.00

Smith & Wesson Model 3000 Slug

Similar to the Model 3000 except: 22" slug barrel; rifle sights; swivels
Estimated Value: $200.00 - $270.00

Smith & Wesson Model 3000 Waterfowler

Similar to the Model 3000 except: steel receiver; 30" full choke barrel; Parkerized finish; dull, oil-finished wood; camouflaged sling & swivels; add $25.00 for "Multi-Choke" system
Estimated Value: $240.00 - $320.00

Smith & Wesson Model 3000 Police

Similar to the Model 3000 except: 18" or 20" slug or cylinder bore barrel; blued or Parkerized finish; bead or rifle sights; walnut finish, hardwood stock & grooved slide handle; or plastic pistol grip & slide handle; or folding stock; add 10% for rifle sights; add 5% for plastic pistol grip and slide handle; add 25% folding stock
Estimated Value: $185.00 - $250.00

Stevens

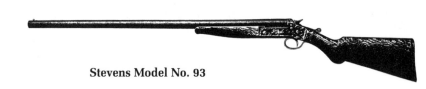

Stevens Model No. 93

Stevens Models No. 93, 97 Nitro Special
Gauge: 12 or 16
Action: Top lever, break-open; exposed hammer; single shot
Magazine: None, single shot
Barrel: Special steel; 28", 30", or 32"
Finish: Blued or nickel plated, case hardened receiver; plain walnut pistol grip stock & lipped forearm
Estimated Value: $60.00 - $80.00

Stevens Model No. 97 Nitro Special

Stevens Models No. 100, 110, & 120
Gauge: 12, 16, or 20
Action: Top lever, break-open; automatic ejector; exposed hammer; single shot
Magazine: None
Barrel: 28", 30", or 32"
Finish: Blued; case hardened receiver; walnut pistol grip stock & forearm; No. 100 no checkering; 110 & 120 checkered walnut
Estimated Value: $65.00 - $85.00

Stevens Model No. 120

Stevens Model No. 140
Similar to the Model 120 except: hammerless & has an automatic safety
Estimated Value: $85.00 - $110.00

Stevens Model No. 140

Stevens Model No. 170

Stevens Model No. 180

Stevens Model No. 182 Trap Gun
Similar to Model No. 180 except:
Trap Grade; 12 gauge only; matted
top of barrel; scroll work on frame
Estimated Value: $110.00 - $150.00

Stevens Models No. 160, 165, or 170
Gauge: 12, 16, or 20
Action: Break-open; exposed
hammer; single shot; automatic
ejector except on 160
Magazine: None; single shot
Barrel: 26", 28", 30", or 32"
Finish: Blued; case hardened
receiver; checkered walnut pistol
grip stock & forearm except 160,
which is plain
Estimated Value: $60.00 - $80.00

Stevens Model No. 180
Gauge: 12, 16, or 20
Action: Top lever, break-open;
hammerless; automatic ejector
Magazine: None; single shot
Barrel: 26", 28", or 30" modified; 32"
or 36" full choke
Finish: Blued; case hardened
receiver; checkered walnut pistol
grip stock & forearm
Estimated Value: $80.00 - $100.00

Stevens Model No. 182 Trap Gun

Stevens Model No. 185, 190, 195
Gauge: 12
Action: Top lever, break-open;
hammerless; automatic shell ejector;
single shot
Magazine: None
Barrel: Round with octagon breech;
30" or 32"
Finish: Blued; case hardened frame;
checkered walnut pistol grip stock &
forearm; receiver engraved on No.
190 & 195
Estimated Value: $110.00 - $150.00

Stevens Model No. 970
Similar to the 185; a 12 gauge made
from around 1912 to 1918
Estimated Value: $70.00 - $90.00

Stevens Model No. 195

Stevens Model No. 970

Stevens

Stevens Model No. 85 Dreadnaught

Stevens Model No. 85 Dreadnaught
Gauge: 12
Action: Top lever, break-open; exposed hammer
Magazine: None, single shot
Barrel: 28", 30", or 32"; full choke
Finish: Blued; case hardened receiver; plain walnut pistol grip stock & lipped forearm
Estimated Value: $65.00 - $80.00

Stevens Model No. 89 Dreadnaught
Same as the No. 85 except: automatic ejector
Estimated Value: $70.00 - $85.00

Stevens Model No. 89 Dreadnaught

Stevens Model No. 106

Stevens Model No. 106
Gauge: 410
Action: Top lever, break-open; exposed hammer; single shot
Magazine: None
Barrel: 26" or 30"
Finish: Blued; case hardened receiver; plain walnut pistol grip stock & forearm
Estimated Value: $60.00 - $80.00

Stevens Model No. 108
Same as the No. 106 except: automatic ejector
Estimated Value: $65.00 - $85.00

Stevens Springfield Model No. 958
Similar to Model No. 108; made from mid-1920's to early 1930's
Estimated Value: $60.00 - $80.00

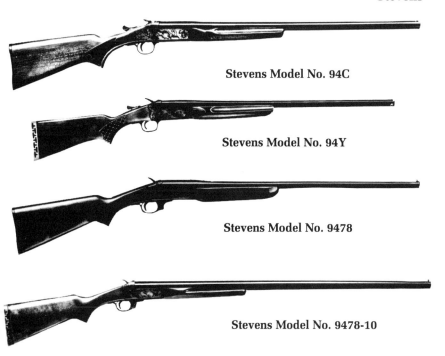

Stevens Model No. 94C

Stevens Model No. 94Y

Stevens Model No. 9478

Stevens Model No. 9478-10

Stevens Model No. 94, 94C
Gauge: 12, 16, 20, or 410
Action: Top lever, break-open; exposed hammer
Magazine: None; single shot
Barrel: 26", 28", 30", 32", or 36"; full choke
Finish: Blued; case hardened receiver; checkered or plain walnut semi-pistol grip stock & grooved forearm
Estimated Value: $65.00 - $85.00

Stevens Model No. 94Y
Similar to 94C except: youth version; shorter stock; recoil pad; 26" barrel; 20 gauge modified or 410 full choke
Estimated Value: $60.00 - $80.00

Stevens Model No. 9478
Similar to the Model 94C except: lever release on the trigger guard; no checkering; add 10% for 36" barrel
Estimated Value: $60.00 - $80.00

Stevens Model No. 9478-10, Waterfowl
Similar to the Model 9478 except: 10 gauge only; 36" full choke barrel; recoil pad
Estimated Value: $80.00 - $100.00

Stevens Model No. 9478-Y
Similar to the Model 9478 except: 410 full or 20 modified gauges; 26" barrel; short stock with rubber buttplate
Estimated Value: $65.00 - $80.00

Stevens

Stevens Models No. 105, 107, 115, & 125
Gauge: 12, 16, 20, or 28
Action: Top lever, break-open; exposed hammer; single shot; automatic ejector on all except Model 105
Magazine: None, single shot
Barrel: 26" or 28"
Finish: Blued; case hardened receiver; checkered or plain walnut semi-pistol grip stock & forearm
Estimated Value: $70.00 - $85.00

Stevens Model No. 125

Stevens Springfield Model No. 95
Similar to the Model 107 with plain stock and forearm
Estimated Value: $60.00 - $80.00

Stevens Model No. 107

Stevens Model No. 115

Stevens Models No. 116 & 117
Similar to the Model 115 with automatic ejector. Model No. 117 is equipped with Lyman sights
Estimated Value: $70.00 - $90.00

Stevens Model No. 116

Stevens Models No. 235, 255, & 265
Gauge: 12 or 16
Action: Box lock; top lever, break-open; exposed hammers; double triggers
Magazine: None
Barrel: Double barrel (side by side); 28", 30, or 32"; matted rib
Finish: Blued; checkered walnut pistol grip stock & forearm; case hardened receiver
Estimated Value: $160.00 - $210.00

Stevens Model No. 235

Stevens Model No. 255

Stevens Model No. 250

Stevens Model No. 250
Gauge: 12
Action: Top lever, break-open; exposed hammer; double trigger
Magazine: None
Barrel: double barrel (side by side); 28", 30", or 32"
Finish: Blued; checkered walnut pistol grip stock & forearm
Estimated Value: $165.00 - $225.00

Stevens Model No. 350

Stevens Models No. 260 & 270
Similar to Model 250 except: special Damascus or twist barrels; 12 or 16 gauge
Estimated Value: $150.00 - $200.00

Stevens Models No. 350, 360, & 370
Gauge: 12 or 16
Action: Top lever, break-open; hammerless; double trigger
Magazine: None
Barrel: Double barrel (side by side); matted rib, 28", 30", or 32"
Finish: Blued; checkered walnut pistol grip stock & forearm
Estimated Value: $140.00 - $180.00

Stevens

Stevens Models No. 355, 365, 375, & 385
Gauge: 12 or 16
Action: Top lever, break-open; hammerless; double trigger
Magazine: None
Barrel: Double barrel (side by side); Krupp steel; matted rib; 28", 30", or 32"
Finish: Blued; checkered walnut straight or pistol grip stock & forearm; 355 & 365 plain; 375 some engraving; 385 engraved receiver
Estimated Value: $150.00 - $200.00

Stevens Model No. 355

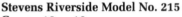

Stevens Model No. 385

Stevens Riverside Model No. 215
Gauge: 12 or 16
Action: Top lever, break-open; exposed hammer; double trigger
Magazine: None
Barrel: Double barrel (side by side); 26", 28", 30", or 32"; full and modified choke; matted rib
Finish: Blued; case hardened receiver; checkered walnut pistol grip stock & forearm
Estimated Value: $150.00 - $200.00

Stevens Riverside Model No. 215

Stevens Riverside Model No. 315

Stevens Riverside Model No. 315
Gauge: 12 or 16
Action: Top lever, break-open; hammerless; double trigger
Magazine: None
Barrel: Double barrel (side by side); 26", 28", 30", or 32"; full and modified choke; matted rib
Finish: Blued; case hardened receiver; checkered walnut semi-pistol grip stock & forearm
Estimated Value: $150.00 - $195.00

Stevens Model No. 335

Stevens Model No. 345

Stevens Model No. 335
Similar to the 315; produced from around 1912 to 1930
Estimated Value: $135.00 - $180.00

Stevens Model No. 345
Similar to the No. 335 except: 20 gauge
Estimated Value: $150.00 - $200.00

Pocket Guide to Shotguns

Stevens Model No. 330

Stevens Model No. 330
Gauge: 12, 16, 20, or 410
Action: Top lever, break-open; hammerless; double trigger; takedown model
Magazine: None
Barrel: Double barrel (side by side); 26"-32"; modified and full choke; full choke in 410
Finish: Blued; case hardened receiver; checkered black walnut pistol grip stock & forearm
Estimated Value: $140.00 - $185.00

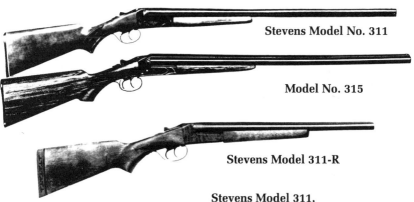

Stevens Model No. 311

Model No. 315

Stevens Model 311-R

Stevens Springfield Model No. 315
A higher quality version of the Model 311
Estimated Value: $190.00 - $240.00

Stevens Model 311-R
A law enforcement version of the Model 311 with 18¼" cylinder bore barrel; recoil pad; 12 gauge only
Estimated Value: $175.00 - $220.00

Stevens Model 311,
Stevens Springfield Model No. 311
Springfield Hammerless
Gauge: 12, 16, 20, or 410
Action: Top lever, break-open; hammerless; double trigger; or single selective trigger; add 10% for single selective trigger; takedown model
Magazine: None
Barrel: Double barrel (side by side); 24"-32"; modified and full choke; except 32" 12 gauge is full choke & 410 ga. full choke; matted rib
Finish: Blued; case hardened receiver; smooth walnut semi-pistol grip stock & forearm
Estimated Value: $180.00 - $225.00

Stevens

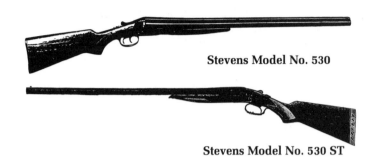

Stevens Model No. 530

Stevens Model No. 530 ST

Model No. 530M

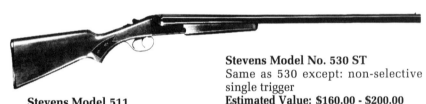

Stevens Model 511

Stevens Model No. 530 ST
Same as 530 except: non-selective
single trigger
Estimated Value: $160.00 - $200.00

Stevens Model No. 530M
Same as 530 except: plastic stock
Estimated Value: $120.00 - $160.00

Stevens Model No. 530
Gauge: 12, 16, 20, or 410
Action: Box lock; top lever, break-open; hammerless; double trigger
Magazine: None
Barrel: Double barrel (side by side); 26"-32"; modified and full choke; except 32" 12 gauge is full choke & 410 ga. full choke
Finish: Blued; case hardened frame; checkered walnut pistol grip stock & forearm; recoil pad on early model
Estimated Value: $155.00 - $195.00

Stevens Model 511
Gauge: 12 or 20; regular or magnum
Action: Box lock; top lever, break-open; double trigger
Magazine: None
Barrel: Double barrel (side by side); 28" modified & full choke
Finish: Blued; checkered hardwood semi-pistol grip stock & small forearm; case hardened receiver
Estimated Value: $150.00 - $200.00

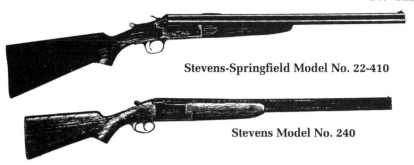

Stevens-Springfield Model No. 22-410

Stevens Model No. 240

**Stevens-Springfield
Model No. 22-410**
Gauge: 410 & 22 caliber rifle
Action: Top lever, break-open;
exposed hammer; single trigger;
separate extractors
Magazine: None
Barrel: 24" Over & under double
barrel; 22 rifle over 410 shotgun
Finish: Blued; case hardened
receiver; plastic semi-pistol grip
stock & forearm; open rear, ramp
front sight
Estimated Value: $110.00 - $140.00

Stevens Model No. 240
Gauge: 410
Action: Top lever, break-open;
exposed hammer; double trigger;
takedown
Magazine: None
Barrel: Over & under double barrel;
both barrels 26" full choke
Finish: Blued; checkered plastic or
wood pistol grip stock & forearm
Estimated Value: $260.00 - $320.00

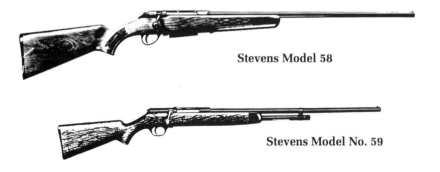

Stevens Model 58

Stevens Model No. 59

Stevens Model No. 58
Gauge: 410
Action: Bolt-action
Magazine: 3-shot detachable box
Barrel: 24"; full choke
Finish: Blued; plain or walnut one-
piece pistol grip stock & forearm
Estimated Value: $65.00 - $85.00

Stevens Model No. 59
Similar to No. 58 except: 5-shot
tubular magazine
Estimated Value: $80.00 - $100.00

Stevens

Stevens-Springfield Model 38

Stevens-Springfield Model 39

Stevens-Springfield Model 38
Similar to Stevens Model No. 58;
made 1939 to 1947
Estimated Value: $65.00 - $80.00

Stevens-Springfield Model 39
Similar to Stevens Model No. 59;
made 1939 to 1947
Estimated Value: $70.00 - $90.00

Stevens Model No. 258

Stevens-Springfield Model No. 37

Stevens Model No. 258
Gauge: 20
Action: Bolt action; repeating
Magazine: 2-shot detachable box
Barrel: 26"; full choke
Finish: Blued; plain walnut one-
piece pistol grip stock & forearm
Estimated Value: $65.00 - $85.00

Stevens Model No. 254
A single shot version of the Model
258
Estimated Value: $50.00 - $65.00

Stevens-Springfield Model 238
Similar to Stevens Model 258; made
1939 to 1947
Estimated Value: $70.00 - $90.00

Stevens-Springfield Model 237
Similar to Stevens Model No. 254;
made from 1939 to 1942
Estimated Value: $55.00 - $70.00

Stevens-Springfield Model No. 37
Similar to Stevens-Springfield Model
237 except: 410 bore; made from
1939 to 1942
Estimated Value: $60.00 - $75.00

Stevens Model No. 124

Stevens Model No. 124
Gauge: 12
Action: Semi-automatic; side ejection; hammerless
Magazine: 2-shot tubular
Barrel: 28"; improved cylinder, modified or full choke
Finish: Blued; checkered plastic pistol grip stock & forearm
Estimated Value: $100.00 - $125.00

Stevens Model No. 520

Stevens Model No. 522

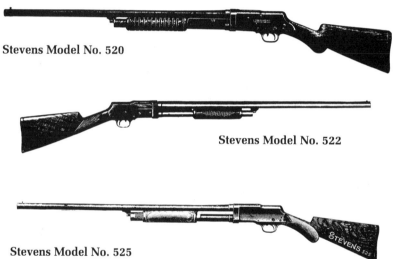

Stevens Model No. 525

Stevens Models No. 520, 521, & 522
Gauge: 12
Action: Browning patent; slide action; takedown; side ejection; hammerless
Magazine: 5-shot tubular
Barrel: 26"-32"; full, modified, or cylinder choke; matted rib on 521
Finish: Blued; walnut pistol grip stock & grooved slide handle; checkered straight grip & slide handle on 522
Estimated Value: $145.00 - $180.00

Stevens Model No. 535

Stevens Models No. 525, 530, & 535
Similar to 520 except fancier grades; 525 is custom built; 530 custom built with engraved receiver & rib; 535 custom built, heavily engraved; add 30% for engraving
Estimated Value: $170.00 - $225.00

Stevens

Stevens Model No. 200

Stevens Model No. 620

Stevens Model No. 620-P

Stevens Model No. 620
Gauge: 12, 16, or 20
Action: Slide action; hammerless;
side ejection; take down model
Magazine: 5-shot tubular
Barrel: 26"-32"; full, modified, or
cylinder bore
Finish: Blued; checkered walnut
pistol grip stock & slide handle
Estimated Value: $140.00 - $185.00

Stevens Model No. 200
Gauge: 20
Action: Pedersen patent, slide
action; hammerless; side ejection;
takedown
Magazine: 5-shot tubular
Barrel: 26"-32"; full , modified, or
cylinder bore
Finish: Blued; walnut pistol grip
stock & grooved slide handle
Estimated Value: $150.00 - $190.00

Stevens Model No. 620-P
Same as Model No. 620 with"Poly-
Choke"
Estimated Value: $150.00 - $190.00

Stevens Model No. 621
Same as Model No. 620 except:
matted rib
Estimated Value: $150.00 - $195.00

Stevens Model No. 77

Stevens Model No. 77
Gauge: 12 or 16
Action: Slide action; hammerless;
side ejection
Magazine: 5-shot tubular
Barrel: 26" or 28"; improved
cylinder, modified or full choke
Finish: Blued; plain walnut pistol
grip stock & grooved slide handle
Estimated Value: $145.00 - $180.00

Stevens Model No. 77-SC
Same as No. 77 except: Savage
"Super Choke" & recoil pad
Estimated Value: $150.00 - $190.00

Pocket Guide to Shotguns

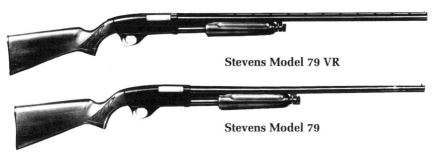

Stevens Model 79 VR

Stevens Model 79

Stevens Model 79 VR
Similar to the Model 79 except:
ventilated rib
Estimated Value: $150.00 - $190.00

Stevens Model 79 Slug
Similar to the Model 79 except: 21"
slug barrel; rifle sights
Estimated Value: $140.00 - $175.00

Stevens Model No. 79
Gauge: 12, 20, or 410; regular or magnum
Action: Slide action; hammerless; side ejection, repeating
Magazine: 4-shot tubular; 3-shot in magnum
Barrel: 28" modified or 30" full in 12 gauge; 28" modified or full in 20 gauge; 26" full in 410
Finish: Blued; checkered hardwood semi-pistol grip stock & fluted slide handle
Estimated Value: $135.00 - $170.00

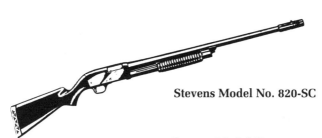

Stevens Model No. 820-SC

Stevens Model No. 820
Gauge: 12
Action: Slide action; hammerless; side ejection
Magazine: 5-shot tubular
Barrel: 28"; improved cylinder, modified or full choke
Finish: Blued; plain walnut semi-pistol grip stock & grooved slide handle
Estimated Value: $140.00 - $175.00

Stevens Model No. 820-SC
Same as No. 820 except: Savage "Super Choke"
Estimated Value: $150.00 - $200.00

Stevens

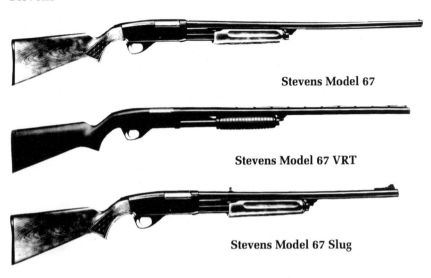

Stevens Model 67

Stevens Model 67 VRT

Stevens Model 67 Slug

Stevens Model 67 Slug
Similar to the Model 67 except: 21"
slug barrel & rifle sights; 12 gauge
only
Estimated Value: $135.00 - $170.00

Stevens Models 67 & 67T
Gauge: 12, 20, or 410; regular or
magnum
Action: Slide action; hammerless;
side ejecting; repeating
Magazine: 4-shot tubular; 3-shot in
magnum
Barrel: 28" modified or full; 26" full in
410; 30" full in 12 gauge; add 10% for
the 67T which has interchangeable
choke tubes in 12 & 20 gauge only
Finish: Blued; hardwood, semi-
pistol grip stock & fluted or grooved
slide handle; some with recoil pad
Estimated Value: $130.00 - $165.00

Stevens Model 67VRT-K
Similar to the Model 67VR-T except:
laminated camo stock; add 8% for
interchangable choke tubes
Estimated Value: $140.00 - $190.00

Stevens Model 67T-Y, 67VRT-Y
Gauge: 20
Action: Slide action; hammerless;
repeating
Magazine: 4-shot
Barrel: 22" with three interchangeable choke tubes; deduct 10% for
plain barrel on 67T-Y; ventilated rib
on 67VRT-Y
Finish: Blued; hardwood, semi-
pistol grip stock & grooved slide
handle; designed for the young
shooter
Estimated Value: $140.00 - $175.00

Stevens Models 67 VR & 67 VRT
Similar to the Model 67 except:
ventilated rib (67 VR); ventilated rib
& interchangeable choke tubes (67
VRT); add 7% for interchangeable
choke tubes in 12 or 20 gauge only
Estimated Value: $150.00 - $185.00

Universal Model 101

Universal Model 101
Gauge: 12
Action: Box lock; top lever, break-open; exposed hammer; single shot
Magazine: None
Barrel: 28" or 30"; full choke
Finish: Blued; plain wood pistol grip stock & tapered forearm
Estimated Value: $70.00 - $90.00

Universal Single Wing
Similar to the Model 101; made from the early to mid-1970's
Estimated Value: $75.00 - $95.00

Universal Model 202

Universal Double Wing

Universal Double Wing
Similar to the Model 202 except: 12 or 20 gauge magnum; recoil pad
Estimated Value: $160.00 - $200.00

Universal Model 202
Gauge: 12, 20, or 410; add 10% for 410 ga.
Action: Box lock; top lever, break-open; hammerless; double triggers
Magazine: None
Barrel: Double barrel (side by side); 26" improved cylinder & modified chokes; 28" modified & full chokes
Finish: Blued; checkered walnut pistol grip stock & forearm
Estimated Value: $150.00 - $185.00

Universal Model 203
Similar to the Model 202 except: 10 gauge; 32" full choke barrels
Estimated Value: $170.00 - $210.00

Universal Model 2030
Similar to the Double Wing except: 10 gauge; 32" full choke barrels
Estimated Value: $175.00 - $220.00

Universal

Universal Over Wing

Universal Auto Wing

Universal Duck Wing

Universal Over Wing
Gauge: 12 or 20
Action: Box lock; top lever, break-open; hammerless; single or double trigger; add 15% for single trigger
Magazine: None
Barrel: Over & under double barrel; 26", 28", or 30"; ventilated rib
Finish: Blued; checkered walnut pistol grip stock & forearm; recoil pad; engraving
Estimated Value: $300.00 - $375.00

Universal Auto Wing
Gauge: 12
Action: Semi-automatic
Magazine: 5-shot tubular
Barrel: 26", 28", or 30"; variety of chokes; ventilated rib
Finish: Blued; checkered walnut pistol grip stock & forearm; sights
Estimated Value: $190.00 - $250.00

Universal Duck Wing
Similar to the Auto Wing except: 28" or 30" full choke; teflon coated barrel
Estimated Value: $210.00 - $275.00

Valmet

Valmet Model 412KE

Valmet Model 412 KE
Gauge: 12
Action: Top lever, break-open;
hammerless; automatic ejectors
Magazine: None
Barrel: Over & under double barrel;
26" improved cylinder & modified;
28" modified & full; 30" modified &
full in 12 gauge; ventilated rib
Finish: Blued; checkered walnut
pistol grip stock & forearm; Monte
Carlo stock with recoil pad; swivels;
interchangeable barrels available to
make it a combination shotgun/rifle
or a double rifle
Estimated Value: $420.00 - $560.00

Valmet Model 412K
Similar to the Model 412KE except:
36" barrels
Estimated Value: $420.00 - $560.00

Valmet Model 412KE Skeet
Similar to the Model 412KE except:
26" or 28" cylinder bore & improved
cylinder bore or skeet choke barrels
Estimated Value: $480.00 - $600.00

Valmet Model 412K Combination
Similar to the Model 412K except:
24" barrels; 12 gauge improved
modified barrel over a rifle barrel in
caliber 222, 223, 243, 30-06, or 308
Estimated Value: $470.00 - $625.00

Valmet Model 412KE Trap
Similar to the Model 412KE except:
30" improved modified & full choke
barrels
Estimated Value: $480.00 - $600.00

Valmet

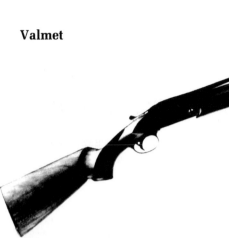

Valmet Model 412S

Valmet 12 Gauge
Gauge: 12
Action: Box lock; top lever, break-open; single selective trigger
Magazine: None
Barrel: Over & under double barrel; 26" improved cylinder & modified; 28" modified & full; 30" modified & full or full & full chokes
Finish: Blued; checkered walnut pistol grip stock & wide forearm
Estimated Value: $320.00 - $425.00

Valmet Model 412S
Gauge: 12 or 20; regular or magnum
Action: Top lever, break-open; hammerless; automatic ejectors; extractor on 36" model
Magazine: None
Barrel: Over & under double barrel; 26" cylinder bore & improved cylinder, improved cylinder or modified; 28" cylinder bore & modified or modified & full; 30" improved modified & full, modified & full; 36" full; ventilated rib
Finish: Blued; checkered walnut pistol grip stock & forearm, adjustable for barrel differences; buttplate adjusts to fit shooter
Estimated Value: $575.00 - $720.00

Valmet Model 412S Combination

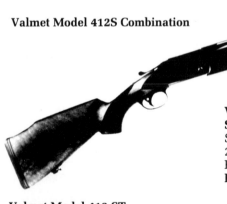

Valmet Model 412 ST
Standard Trap
Similar to the Model 412S except: Monte Carlo stock, 12 gauge only, 30" or 32" barrels; add 30% for Premium Grade Model
Estimated Value: $690.00 - $860.00

Valmet Model 412ST
Standard Skeet
Similar to the Model 412S except: 28" skeet choke barrels; add 30% for Premium Grade Model
Estimated Value: $690.00 - $860.00

Valmet Model 412S Combination
Similar to the Model 412S except: 24" barrels; 12 gauge improved modified barrel over a 222, 223, 243, 30-06 or 308 caliber rifle barrel
Estimated Value: $660.00 - $825.00

Pocket Guide to Shotguns

Weatherby Regency

Weatherby Regency
Gauge: 12 or 20
Action: Box lock; top lever, break-open; hammerless; automatic ejectors; single selective trigger
Magazine: None
Barrel: Over & under double barrel; 26", 28", or 30"; variety of chokes; ventilated rib
Finish: Blued; checkered walnut pistol grip stock & fluted forearm; recoil pad
Estimated Value: $740.00 - $925.00

Weatherby Regency Skeet
Similar to the Regency except: skeet chokes; 26" or 28" barrels
Estimated Value: $780.00 - $975.00

Weatherby Regency Trap
Similar to the Regency except: wide ventilated rib; 30" or 32" full & full, full & improved modified, or full & modified chokes; choice of regular or Monte Carlo stock; 12 gauge only
Estimated Value: $800.00 - $1,000.00

Weatherby Olympian

Weatherby Olympian
Gauge: 12 or 20
Action: Box lock; top lever, break-open; selective automatic ejectors
Magazine: None
Barrel: Over & under double barrel; 26" or 28" full & modified; 26" or 28" modified & improved cylinder; 30" full & modified; ventilated rib
Finish: Blued; checkered walnut pistol grip stock & fluted forearm; recoil pad
Estimated Value: $525.00 - $700.00

Weatherby Olympian Skeet
Similar to the Olympian except: 26" or 28" skeet choke barrels
Estimated Value: $620.00 - $775.00

Weatherby Olympian Trap
Similar to the Olympian except: ventilated rib on top and between barrels; 30" or 32" barrels; full & modified or full & improved modified chokes; Monte Carlo or regular stock
Estimated Value: $640.00 - $800.00

Weatherby

Weatherby Orion

Weatherby Orion Trap
Similar to the Orion except: 12 gauge only; 30" or 32" full & improved modified or full & modified barrels; wide rib ventilated rib on top and between barrels; Monte Carlo or regular stock
Estimated Value: $760.00 - $950.00

Weatherby Orion Skeet
Similar to the Orion except: 26" skeet choke barrels; 12 or 20 gauge
Estimated Value: $730.00 - $910.00

Weatherby Orion Grade I & Grade III
Gauge: 12, 20, 28, or 410
Action: Box lock; top lever, break-open; selective automatic ejectors; single selective trigger
Magazine: None
Barrel: Over & under double barrel; 26" or 28" modified & improved cylinder; 28" or 30" full & modified; ventilated rib; multi-choke after 1983
Finish: Blued; checkered walnut pistol grip stock & fluted forearm; rosewood cap at grip; recoil pad; engraved receiver; high-lustre finish; add 28% for Grade III
Estimated Value: $630.00 - $790.00

Weatherby Athena

Weatherby Athena Grade IV & Grade V
Gauge: 12, 20, 28, or 410
Action: Box lock; top lever, break-open; selective automatic ejectors; single selective trigger
Magazine: None
Barrel: Over & under double barrel; 26" or 28" modified & improved cylinder; 28" modified & full choke; ventilated rib on top & between barrels; multi-choke after 1983
Finish: Blued; special selected checkered walnut pistol grip stock & fluted forearm; high-lustre finish; rosewood grip cap; recoil pad; silver gray engraved receiver; add 28% for Grade V
Estimated Value: $1,175.00 - $1,460.00

Weatherby Athena Trap
Similar to the Athena except: 12 gauge only; 30" or 32" full & improved modified or full & modified barrels; wide ventilated rib; with center bead sight; Monte Carlo stock
Estimated Value: $1,185.00 - $1,480.00

Weatherby Athena Skeet
Similar to the Athena except: 26" skeet choke barrels
Estimated Value: $1,180.00 - $1,470.00

Weatherby Athena Single Barrel Trap
Similar guality and workmanship to the Athena Trap; with a single ventilated rib barrel
Estimated Value: $1,185.00 - $1,480.00

Weatherby Patrician

Weatherby Patrician Deluxe

Weatherby Patrician & Patrician II
Gauge: 12; regular (Patrician); 12 magnum (Patrician II)
Action: Slide action; hammerless; side ejection
Magazine: 2-shot Tubular with plug
Barrel: 26", 28", or 30"; variety of chokes; ventilated rib; add 10% for Trap models
Finish: Blued; checkered walnut pistol grip stock & grooved slide handle; recoil pad
Estimated Value: $240.00 - $300.00

Weatherby Patrician Deluxe
Similar to the Patrician except: decorated satin silver receiver & higher quality wood
Estimated Value: $310.00 - $390.00

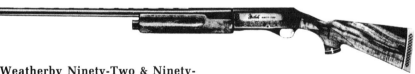

Weatherby Ninety-Two

Weatherby Ninety-Two & Ninety-Two IMC
Gauge: 12; regular or magnum
Action: Slide action; hammerless
Magazine: 2-shot tubular with plug
Barrel: 26" improved cylinder or skeet, 28" modified or full, 30" full; ventilated rib; multi-choke barrel after 1983
Finish: Blued; checkered walnut pistol grip stock & slide handle; high-gloss finish; rosewood grip cap; etched receiver; recoil pad
Estimated Value: $270.00 - $340.00

Weatherby Ninety-Two Buckmaster
Similar to the Ninety-Two except: 22" slug barrel & rifle sights
Estimated Value: $265.00 - $335.00

Weatherby/Western

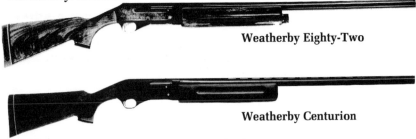

Weatherby Eighty-Two

Weatherby Centurion

Weatherby Centurion & Centurion II
Gauge: 12; regular (Centurion); 12 gauge magnum (Centurion II)
Action: Semi-automatic, gas operated; hammerless
Magazine: Tubular
Barrel: 26", 28", or 30"; variety of chokes; ventilated rib
Finish: Blued; checkered walnut pistol grip stock & grooved forearm; recoil pad; add 8% for Trap model
Estimated Value: $255.00 - $320.00

Weatherby Centurion Deluxe
Similar to the Centurion except: decorated satin silver receiver & higher quality wood
Estimated Value: $285.00 - $360.00

Weatherby Eighty-Two & Eighty-Two IMC
Gauge: 12; regular or magnum
Action: Gas operated, semi-automatic; hammerless
Magazine: 2-shot tubular with plug
Barrel: 26" improved cylinder or skeet, 28" modified or full, 30" full; ventilated rib; "Multi-Choke" barrel after 1983
Finish: Blued; checkered walnut pistol grip stock & forearm; high gloss finish; rosewood grip cap; etched receiver; recoil pad; add 7% for Trap model
Estimated Value: $330.00 - $415.00

Weatherby Eighty-Two Buckmaster
Similar to the Eighty-Two except: 22" slug barrel & rifle sights
Estimated Value: $330.00 - $415.00

Western

Western Long Range
Gauge: 12, 16, 20, or 410
Action: Box lock; top lever, break-open; hammerless; double or single trigger; add 10% for single trigger
Magazine: None
Barrel: Double barrel (side by side); 26" - 32"; modified & full choke
Finish: Blued; plain walnut pistol grip stock & forearm
Estimated Value: $260.00 - $325.00

Western Long Range

Western Field

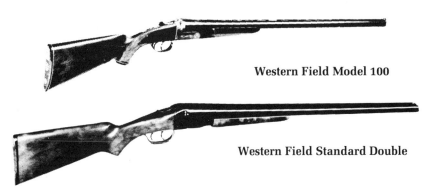

Western Field Model 100

Western Field Standard Double

Western Field Model 100
Gauge: 12, 16, 20, or 410
Action: Box lock; thumb sliding, break-open; hammerless; single shot
Magazine: None
Barrel: 26"-30"; full choke
Finish: Blued; wood semi-pistol grip stock & tapered forearm
Estimated Value: $60.00 - $75.00

Western Field Standard Double
Gauge: 12, 16, 20, or 410
Action: Box lock; top lever, break-open; hammerless
Magazine: None
Barrel: Double barrel (side by side); 26"- 30"; modified & full or full & full chokes; matted rib
Finish: Blued; wood semi-pistol grip stock & short tapered forearm
Estimated Value: $150.00 - $200.00

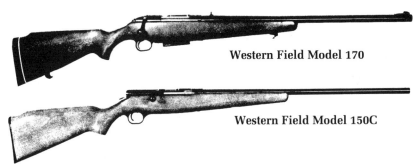

Western Field Model 170

Western Field Model 150C

Western Field Model 150C
Gauge: 410
Action: Bolt action; repeating
Magazine: 3-shot; top loading
Barrel: 25"; full choke; 3" chamber
Finish: Blued; wood Monte Carlo pistol grip one-piece stock & forearm
Estimated Value: $70.00 - $85.00

Western Field Model 170
Gauge: 12
Action: Bolt action; repeating
Magazine: 3-shot detachable clip
Barrel: 28"
Finish: Blued; wood Monte Carlo semi-pistol grip one-piece stock & forearm; recoil pad; sights; swivels
Estimated Value: $70.00 - $90.00

Western Field

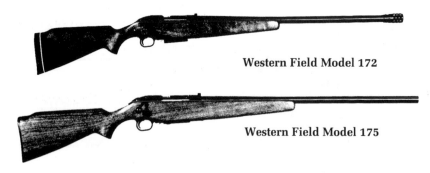

Western Field Model 172

Western Field Model 175

Western Field Bolt Action
Gauge: 12 or 20 (regular or magnum); or 410
Action: Bolt action; repeating
Magazine: 3-shot detachable box; 410 top loading
Barrel: 28"; full choke; 25" in 410
Finish: Blued; smooth walnut finish hardwood one-piece pistol grip stock & forearm
Estimated Value: $75.00 - $90.00

Western Field Model 172
Similar to the Model 170 except: without sights or swivels; adjustable choke
Estimated Value: $65.00 - $80.00

Western Field Model 175
Similar to the Model 172 except: 20 gauge; 26" barrel; without adjustable choke
Estimated Value: $60.00 - $75.00

Western Field Model 550

Western Field Model 550 Deluxe
Gauge: 12 or 20; regular or magnum
Action: Slide action; hammerless; repeating
Magazine: 5-shot tubular; 4-shot magnum
Barrel: 28" with 3 interchangeable "Accu-Choke" tubes; ventilated rib
Finish: Blued; checkered hardwood pistol grip stock & slide handle; chrome damascened finish on bolt; recoil pad; engraved receiver
Estimated Value: $150.00 - $190.00

Western Field Model 550
Gauge: 12 or 20 (regular or magnum); and 410 ga.
Action: Slide action; hammerless; repeating
Magazine: 4-shot magnum, 5-shot regular, tubular
Barrel: 26" (410); 30" in 12 or 20 gauge; full or modified choke; add 10% for variable choke; add 10% for optional ventilated rib
Finish: Blued; smooth hardwood pistol grip stock with fluted comb; grooved slide handle
Estimated Value: $140.00 - $175.00

Winchester

Winchester Model 20

Winchester Model 37

Winchester Model 20
Gauge: 410
Action: Top lever, break-open; exposed hammer
Magazine: None; single shot
Barrel: 26"; full choke
Finish: Blued; plain or checkered wood pistol grip stock & lipped forearm
Estimated Value: $190.00 - $250.00

Winchester Model 37
Gauge: 12, 16, 20, 28, or 410
Action: Top lever, break-open; partial exposed hammer; automatic ejector
Magazine: None; single shot
Barrel: 26"-32"; full or modified choke; or cylinder bore
Finish: Blued; plain walnut semi-pistol grip stock & forearm; add $150.00 for 28 gauge; add $25.00 for 410 gauge
Estimated Value: $165.00 - $210.00

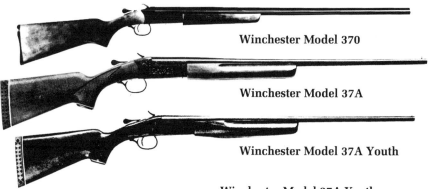

Winchester Model 370

Winchester Model 37A

Winchester Model 37A Youth

Winchester Model 37A Youth
Similar to the 37A except: 26" barrel & shorter stock
Estimated Value: $60.00 - $75.00

Winchester Model 370
Gauge: 12, 16, 20, 28, or 410
Action: Top lever, break-open; exposed hammer; single shot; automatic ejector
Magazine: None; single shot
Barrel: 26"-32" or 36" full choke; modified in 20 gauge
Finish: Blued; plain wood semi-pistol grip stock & forearm
Estimated Value: $75.00 - $90.00

Winchester Model 37A
Similar to the Model 370 except: also with 36" Waterfowl barrel; add $5.00 for 36" barrel; checkered stock; fluted forearm; engraved receiver; gold-plated trigger
Estimated Value: $65.00 - $85.00

Winchester

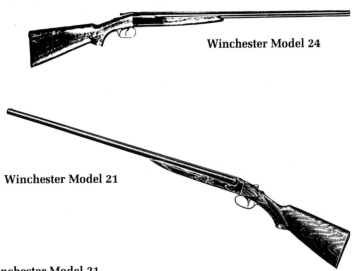

Winchester Model 24

Winchester Model 21

Winchester Model 21
Gauge: 12, 16, or 20
Action: Box lock; top lever, break-open; hammerless, double or single trigger
Magazine: None
Barrel: 26-32" double barrel (side by side); matted or ventilated rib; full, modified or cylinder bore
Finish: Checkered walnut, pistol grip stock & forearm
Estimated Value: $2,000.00 - $2,500.00

Winchester Model 24
Gauge: 12, 16, or 20
Action: Box lock; top lever, break-open; hammerless, automatic ejectors; double triggers
Magazine: None
Barrel: Double barrel (side by side), 28" cylinder bore & modified in 12 gauge; other gauges modified & full choke; raised matted rib
Finish: Blued; plain or checkered walnut pistol grip stock & forearm
Estimated Value: $265.00 - $350.00

Winchester Model 23 Custom
Gauge: 12
Action: Box lock; top lever, break-open; hammerless, single selective trigger
Magazine: None
Barrel: Double barrel (side by side), 25½" "Winchoke"
Finish: Blued; checkered walnut, pistol grip stock & forearm
Estimated Value: $1,180.00 - $1,480.00

Winchester Model 23 Classic
Similar to the Model 23 Custom except: 26" barrels; 12, 20 or 28 gauge improved cylinder & modified; 410 modified & full choke; engraving on receiver; add 5% for 28 gauge or 410 bore
Estimated Value: $1,180.00 - $1,480.00

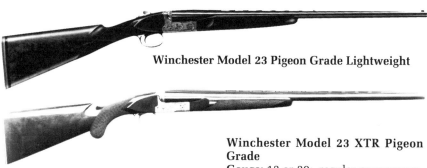

Winchester Model 23 Pigeon Grade Lightweight

Winchester Model 23XTR Pigeon Grade

Winchester Model 23 Pigeon Grade Lightweight

Similar to the Model 23 XTR Pigeon Grade except: lighter weight; straight grip stock; rubber butt pad; 25½" barrels
Estimated Value: $800.00 - $1,065.00

Winchester Model 23 XTR Pigeon Grade

Gauge: 12 or 20; regular or magnum
Action: Box lock; top lever, break-open; hammerless; selective automatic ejectors; single trigger
Magazine: None
Barrel: Double barrel (side by side); 26" improved cylinder & modified; 28" modified & full choke; tapered ventilated rib; Winchoke after 1980
Finish: Blued; checkered walnut semi-pistol grip stock & forearm; silver gray engraved receiver
Estimated Value: $820.00 - $1,095.00

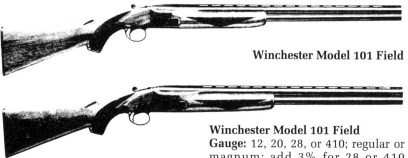

Winchester Model 101 Field

Winchester Model 101 Skeet

Winchester Model 101 Skeet

Similar to the Model 101 except: skeet stock & chokes; add 3% for 410 or 28 gauge
Estimated Value: $750.00 - $1,000.00

Winchester Model 101 Field

Gauge: 12, 20, 28, or 410; regular or magnum; add 3% for 28 or 410 gauge; add $10.00 for magnum
Action: Box lock; top lever, break-open; hammerless; single trigger; automatic ejector
Magazine: None
Barrel: Over & under double barrel; 26"-30"; various choke combinations; ventilated rib
Finish: Blued; checkered walnut pistol grip stock & wide forearm; recoil pad on magnum; engraved receiver
Estimated Value: $700.00 - $940.00

Winchester

Winchester Xpert Model 96

Winchester Model 101 Trap
Similar to the Model 101 except: regular or Monte Carlo stock; recoil pad; 30" or 32" barrels; 12 gauge only
Estimated Value: $760.00 - $1,020.00

Winchester Xpert Model 96
A lower priced version of the Model 101; no engraving; also lacking some of the internal & external extras
Estimated Value: $490.00 - $650.00

Winchester Xpert Model 96 Trap
Similar to the Xpert Model 96 except: Monte Carlo stock; 30" barrel
Estimated Value: $500.00 - $675.00

Winchester Model 101 Lightweight Winchoke

Winchester Model 101 Waterfowl Winchoke

Winchester Model 101 Waterfowler
Similar to the Model 101 Waterfowl Winchoke with sandblasted blued finish & low-lustre wood finish
Estimated Value: $940.00 - $1,180.00

Winchester Model 101 Lightweight Winchoke
Similar to the Model 101 Field except: interchangeable choke tube system; lighter weight; ventilated rib between barrels as well as on top; 12 or 20 gauge
Estimated Value: $840.00 - $1,050.00

Winchester Model 101 Waterfowl Winchoke
Similar to the Model 101 field except: 12 gauge only; 32" barrels; ventilated rib between barrels as well as on top; interchangeable choke tube system; recoil pad
Estimated Value: $690.00 - $920.00

Pocket Guide to Shotguns

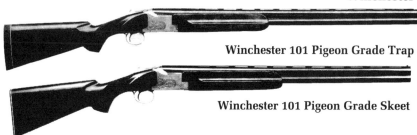

Winchester 101 Pigeon Grade Trap

Winchester 101 Pigeon Grade Skeet

Winchester 101 Pigeon Grade Skeet
Similar to the 101 Pigeon Grade
except: 27" or 28" skeet choke
barrels; front & center sighting beads;
also 410 or 28 gauge available
Estimated Value: $800.00 - $1,000.00

Winchester 101 Pigeon Grade Trap
Similar to the 101 Pigeon Grade
except: 30" or 32" barrels; recoil pad;
regular or Monte Carlo stock
Estimated Value: $760.00 - $975.00

Winchester 101 Pigeon Grade
Gauge: 12 or 20; regular or magnum
Action: Box lock; top lever, break-
open; selective automatic ejectors;
single selective trigger
Magazine: None
Barrel: Over & under double barrel;
26" improved cylinder & modified;
28" modified & full; ventilated rib
Finish: Blued; checkered walnut
pistol grip stock & fluted forearm;
silver gray engraved receiver; recoil
pad on magnum
Estimated Value: $720.00 - $900.00

Winchester Pigeon Grade Featherweight

Winchester Pigeon Grade
Featherweight
Similar to the Pigeon Grade
Lightweight except: 25½" barrels;
improved cylinder & improved
modified or improved cylinder &
modified; straight grip English style
stock; rubber butt pad
Estimated Value: $890.00 - $1,185.00

Winchester Pigeon Grade
Lightweight
Gauge: 12 , 20, or 28
Action: Top lever, break-open;
hammerless; automatic ejectors;
single selective trigger
Magazine: None
Barrel: Over & under double barrel;
27" or 28" interchangeable choke
tubes; ventilated rib on top &
between barrels
Finish: Blued, silver gray stain finish
receiver with etching of gamebirds &
scroll work; checkered walnut
rounded pistol grip stock & fluted
forearm; recoil pad; straight stock
available on 28 gauge
Estimated Value: $1,150.00 - $1,435.00

Winchester Diamond Grade Single Barrel

Winchester Diamond Grade O/U Trap

Winchester Diamond Grade
O/U Skeet

Similar to the Diamond Grade O/U Trap except: 12, 20, 28, or 410 gauge; 27" barrels; add $75.00 for Winchoke

Estimated Value: $1,150.00 - $1,435.00

Winchester Diamond Grade
O/U Trap

Gauge: 12

Action: Top lever, break-open; hammerless; automatic ejectors; single selective trigger

Magazine: None

Barrel: Over & under double barrel; 30" or 32" full choke top, inter-changeable choke tube system bottom; ventilated rib on top & between barrels

Finish: Blued, silver gray stain finish on receiver with engraving; checkered walnut pistol grip stock & lipped forearm; ebony inlay in pistol grip; regular or Monte Carlo stock; recoil pad

Estimated Value: $1,115.00 - $1,395.00

Winchester Diamond Grade
Single Barrel

Similar in guality and workman ship to the Diamond Grade O/U Trap except: with only one 32" or 34" barrel; interchangeable choke tube system; high-ventilated rib

Estimated Value: $1,285.00 - $1,610.00

Winchester Diamond Grade
Combination

Similar to the Diamond Grade O/U Trap except: with a set of 30" or 32" barrels & a 34" high-rib single barrel; lower barrel & single barrel use interchangeable choke tube system

Estimated Value: $1,765.00 - $2,200.00

Winchester Model 501 Grand European Skeet

Winchester Super Grade

**Winchester Super Grade,
Shotgun Rifle**
Gauge: 12; 3" chamber
Caliber: 243 Win., 30-06, 300 Win. mag.
Action: Top lever, break-open; hammerless; automatic ejectors; single selective trigger
Magazine: None
Barrel: Over & under combination; 12 gauge shotgun barrel with interchangeable choke tube system over rifle barrel
Sights: Folding leaf rear, blade front
Finish: Blued; silver gray satin finish engraved receiver; checkered walnut Monte Carlo pistol grip stock & fluted forearm; recoil pad; swivels. A limited production shotgun/rifle combination
Estimated Value: $1,435.00 - $1,910.00

Winchester Model 501 Grand European Trap
Gauge: 12
Action: Top lever, break-open; hammerless; automatic ejectors; single selective trigger
Magazine: None
Barrel: Over & under double barrel; 30" or 32" improved modified & full choke; ventilated rib on top & between barrels
Finish: Blued; silver gray satin finish engraved receiver; checkered walnut pistol grip stock & fluted lipped forearm; regular or Monte Carlo stock; recoil pad
Estimated Value: $975.00 - $1,290.00

Winchester Model 501 Grand European Skeet
Similar to the Model 501 Grand European Trap except: 27" skeet choke barrels; 12 or 20 gauge
Estimated Value: $975.00 - $1,290.00

Winchester

Winchester Model 1901

Winchester Model 36

Winchester Model 41

Winchester Model 97

Winchester Model 41
Gauge: 410
Action: Bolt action; single shot, rear cocking piece
Magazine: None
Barrel: 24"; full choke
Finish: Blued; plain or checkered straight or pistol grip one-piece stock & forearm
Estimated Value: $200.00 - $250.00

Winchester Model 97
Gauge: 12 or 16
Action: Slide action; exposed hammer; repeating
Magazine: 5-shot tubular
Barrel: 26", 28", 30", or 32" modified, full choke or cylinder bore
Finish: Blued; plain wood, semi-pistol grip stock & grooved slide handle; made in Field Grade; add $250.00 for Tournament Grade; add $500.00 for Pigeon Grade
Estimated Value: $360.00 - $450.00

Winchester Model 1901
Gauge: 10
Action: Lever action; repeating
Magazine: 4-shot tubular
Barrel: 30" or 32"; full choke
Finish: Blued; walnut, pistol grip stock & forearm
Estimated Value: $560.00 - $700.00

Winchester Model 36
Gauge: 9mm shot or ball cartridges
Action: Bolt action; single shot; rear cocking piece
Magazine: None
Barrel: 18"; plain
Finish: Blued; straight grip one-piece stock & forearm
Estimated Value: $220.00 - $275.00

Winchester Model 97 Trench

Winchester Model 97 Riot Gun

Winchester Model 97 Riot
Similar to the Model 97 (field grade) except: 20" cylinder bore barrel
Estimated Value: $320.00 - $400.00

Winchester Model 97 Trench
Similar to the 97 Riot Gun with handguard & bayonet; used in World War I
Estimated Value: $480.00 - $600.00

Winchester Model 12 Pre-'65

Winchester Model 12
Gauge: 12, 16, 20, or 28
Action: Slide action; hammerless; repeating
Magazine: 6-shot tubular
Barrel: 26"-32"; standard chokes
Finish: Blued; plain or checkered walnut pistol grip stock & slide handle; some slide handles grooved; made in various grades: Standard, Featherweight, Rib Barrel, Riot Gun, Duck, Skeet, Trap, Pigeon, Super Pigeon from 1912 to about 1964; in 1972 Field Gun, Skeet & Trap were reissued; deduct 50% for guns made after 1971; priced for Standard Grade made before 1964; add $50.00 for ventilated rib; $40.00 for raised matted rib; approximately 50% for Pigeon & approximately 120% for Super Pigeon grades; deduct approximately 25% for Riot Gun
Estimated Value: $550.00 - $675.00

Winchester

Winchester Model 12 Skeet Pre-'65

Winchester Model 12 Trap Pre-'65

Winchester Model 12 Field After '72

Winchester Model 12 Super Pigeon After '72

Winchester Model 12 Trap After '72

Winchester Model 42

Winchester Model 42 Skeet

Winchester Model 42 Skeet
Similar to the Model 42 except:
straight grip stock; matted rib & skeet
choke barrel
Estimated Value: $600.00 - $750.00

Winchester Model 42
Gauge: 410
Action: Slide action; hammerless;
repeating
Magazine: 5-shot tubular
Barrel: 26" or 28"; modified, full
choke or cylinder bore
Finish: Blued; plain walnut pistol
grip stock & grooved slide handle
Estimated Value: $560.00 - $700.00

Winchester Model 42 Deluxe
Similar to the Model 42 except:
higher quality finish; ventilated rib;
select wood; checkering
Estimated Value: $700.00 - $875.00

Winchester Model 25

Winchester Model 25 Riot Gun

Winchester Model 25
Gauge: 12
Action: Slide action; hammerless;
repeating
Magazine: 4-shot tubular
Barrel: 26" or 28"; improved
cylinder, modified or full choke
Finish: Blued; plain walnut semi-
pistol grip stock & grooved slide
handle
Estimated Value: $270.00 - $340.00

Winchester Model 25 Riot Gun
Similar to the Model 25 except: 25"
cylinder bore barrel
Estimated Value: $230.00 - $290.00

Winchester

Winchester Model 1200

Winchester Model 1200 Field
Gauge: 12, 16, or 20; regular or magnum; add $15.00 for magnum
Action: Front lock; rotary bolt; slide action; repeating
Magazine: 4-shot tubular
Barrel: 26"-30"; various chokes or adjustable choke (Winchoke); add $5.00 for adjustable choke; ventilated rib optional; add $25.00 for ventilated rib
Finish: Blued; checkered walnut pistol grip stock & slide handle; recoil pad; alloy receiver
Estimated Value: $175.00 - $220.00

Winchester Model 1200 Deer
Similar to the Model 1200 field except: 22" barrel; rifle sights
Estimated Value: $185.00 - $230.00

Winchester Model 1200 Skeet
Similar to 1200 field except: 12 or 20 gauge only; 26" skeet choke barrel; ventilated rib
Estimated Value: $200.00 - $250.00

Winchester Model 1200 Trap
Similar to the 1200 field except: 30" full choke barrel; ventilated rib; regular or Monte Carlo stock
Estimated Value: $210.00 - $260.00

Winchester Model 1200 Skeet

Winchester Model 1200 & 1300 Defender
Gauge: 12 or 20; regular or magnum
Action: Slide action front lock rotary bolt
Magazine: 6-shot tubular; 5-shot in magnum
Barrel: 18"; cylinder bore; add 7% for optional rifle sights
Finish: Blued; plain wood semi-pistol grip stock & grooved slide handle; a pistol grip model made beginning in 1984
Estimated Value: $155.00 - $190.00

Winchester Model 1200 & 1300 Marine
Same as the Model 1200 Police except: rifle sights
Estimated Value: $260.00 - $325.00

Winchester Model 1200 Police
Same as the Model 1200 Defender except: stainless steel barrel & satin chrome finish on all other external metal parts; also made with shoulder stock or pistol grip (1984); 12 gauge only
Estimated Value: $230.00 - $290.00

Winchester

Winchester Model 1300 XTR

Winchester Model 1300XTR Deer Gun

Winchester Model 1300 XTR
Gauge: 12 or 20; regular or magnum
Action: Slide action; hammerless; repeating
Magazine: 3-shot tubular
Barrel: 26", 28", or 30"; improved cylinder, modified or full choke; ventilated rib optional; add $15.00 for ventilated rib
Finish: Blued; checkered walnut pistol grip stock & slide handle
Estimated Value: $220.00 - $275.00

Winchester Model 1300XTR Deer Gun
Similar to the Model 1300XTR except: 22" slug barrel; rifle sights; sling; recoil pad; 12 gauge only
Estimated Value: $235.00 - $290.00

Winchester Model 1300 Winchoke

Winchester Model 1300 Featherweight
Similar to the Model 1300 Winchoke except: 22" barrel
Estimated Value: $215.00 - $270.00

Winchester Model 1300 Waterfowl
Similar to the Model 1300 Featherweight except: sling swivels, 30" barrel; 12 gauge only; dull finish on some models
Estimated Value: $220.00 - $275.00

Winchester Model 1300 Winchoke
Gauge: 12 or 20 magnum
Action: Slide action; hammerless; repeating
Magazine: 4-shot tubular
Barrel: 26"or 28"; ventilated rib; Winchoke system (changeable choke tubes)
Finish: Blued; checkered walnut straight or pistol grip stock & slide handle; recoil pad on 12 gauge; Ladies' & Youth Model added 1990
Estimated Value: $215.00 - $270.00

Pocket Guide to Shotguns

177

Winchester

Winchester Model 1300
Win-Tuff Deer Gun
Similar to the Model 1300XTR Deer Gun except: rifled barrel; laminated stock or walnut stock and forearm
Estimated Value: $255.00 - $320.00

Winchester Model 1300 Turkey
Similar to the Model 1300 Waterfowl except: 22" barrel; add 5% for optional camo finish; add 5% for National Wild, Turkey Federation Model or Ladies' Model
Estimated Value: $245.00 - $310.00

Winchester Ranger

Winchester Ranger Deer Gun

Winchester Ranger Deer Gun & 1300 Ranger Deer Gun
Similar to the Ranger except: 22" or 24" cylinder bore deer barrel; rifle sights; recoil pad
Estimated Value: $180.00 - $225.00

Winchester Ranger 1300
Deer Combination
Similar to the Ranger except: 24" cylinder bore deer barrel and interchangeable 28" Winchoke barrel
Estimated Value: $210.00 - $265.00

Winchester Ranger & 1300 Ranger
Gauge: 12 or 20; regular or magnum
Action: Slide action; hammerless; side ejecting
Magazine: 4-shot tubular; factory installed plug is removable
Barrel: 28"; ventilated rib optional; add 15% for vent rib; interchangeable choke tubes
Finish: Blued; walnut-finished, semi-pistol grip stock & grooved slide handle; recoil pad
Estimated Value: $170.00 - $215.00

Winchester Ranger Youth, 1300
Ranger Youth
Similar to the Ranger except: 20 gauge; stock & forearm are modified for young shooters; stock can be replaced with regular size stock; 22" modified or Winchoke barrel
Estimated Value: $215.00 - $265.00

Winchester Model 1911

Winchester Model 40
Gauge: 12
Action: Semi-automatic; hammerless
Magazine: 4-shot tubular
Barrel: 28" or 30"; modified or full choke
Finish: Blued; plain walnut pistol grip stock & forearm
Estimated Value: $320.00 - $400.00

Winchester Model 1911
Gauge: 12
Action: Semi-auto; hammerless
Magazine: 4-shot tubular
Barrel: 26"-32"; various chokes
Finish: Blued; plain or checkered semi-pistol grip stock & forearm
Estimated Value: $375.00 - $500.00

Winchester Model 40 Skeet
Similar to the Model 40 except: 24" skeet barrel; checkering; "Cutts Compensator"
Estimated Value: $360.00 - $450.00

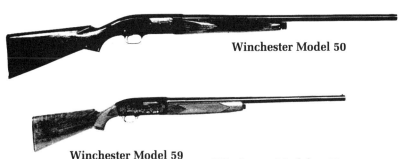

Winchester Model 50

Winchester Model 59

Winchester Model 50
Gauge: 12 or 20
Action: Semi-automatic; non-recoiling barrel; hammerless
Magazine: 2-shot tubular
Barrel: 26"-30"; variety of chokes; ventilated rib optional; add $25.00 for ventilated rib
Finish: Blued; checkered walnut pistol grip stock & forearm
Estimated Value: $280.00 - $350.00

Winchester Model 50 Trap
Similar to the Model 50 except: 12 gauge only; Monte Carlo stock; 30" full choke; ventilated rib
Estimated Value: $335.00 - $420.00

Winchester Model 59
Gauge: 12
Action: Semi-auto; hammerless; non-recoiling barrel
Magazine: 2-shot tubular
Barrel: 26"-30"; variety of chokes; steel & glass fiber composition; interchangeable choke tubes optional
Finish: Blued; checkered walnut pistol grip stock & forearm; alloy receiver
Estimated Value: $300.00 - $380.00

Winchester Model 50 Skeet
Similar to the Model 50 except: skeet stock; 26" skeet choke barrel; ventilated rib
Estimated Value: $335.00 - $420.00

Winchester

Winchester Model 1400 Skeet

Winchester Model 1400 Deer

Winchester Model 1400 Mark II

Winchester Model 1400

Winchester Model 1400 Trap

Winchester Model 1400 & 1400 Winchoke
Gauge: 12, 16, or 20
Action: Semi-automatic, gas operated
Magazine: 2-shot tubular
Barrel: 26", 28", or 30"; variety of chokes; adjustable choke after 1978; ventilated rib optional; add $25.00 for ventilated rib
Finish: Blued; checkered walnut pistol grip stock & forearm; recoil pad; Cycolak stock with recoil reduction system optional until late 1970's; add $25.00 for Cycolak stock
Estimated Value: $190.00 - $250.00

Winchester Model 1400 Mark II
Similar to the Model 1400 except: lighter weight; with minor improvements
Estimated Value: $180.00 - $240.00

Winchester Model 1400 Deer Gun
Similar to the Model 1400 except: 22" slug barrel; rifle sights
Estimated Value: $200.00 - $260.00

Winchester Model 1400 Skeet
Similar to the Model 1400 except: 12 or 20 gauge; 26" barrel; ventilated rib; add $25.00 for recoil reduction system
Estimated Value: $210.00 - $280.00

Winchester Model 1400 Trap
Similar to the Model 1400 except: 12 gauge; 30" full choke barrel; ventilated rib; regular or Monte Carlo stock; add $25.00 for recoil reduction system
Estimated Value: $210.00 - $290.00

Winchester Model 1500 XTR

Winchester Model 1500 XTR

Gauge: 12 or 20; regular or magnum
Action: Semi-automatic, gas operated
Magazine: 3-shot tubular
Barrel: 26", 28", or 30"; improved cylinder, modified or full choke; add $25.00 for optional ventilated rib
Finish: Blued; checkered walnut pistol grip stock & forearm; alloy receiver
Estimated Value: $225.00 - $300.00

Winchester Model 1500 XTR Winchoke

Similar to the Model 1500XTR except: removable choke tube system; 28" barrel only; add $25.00 for ventilated rib
Estimated Value: $240.00 - $320.00

Winchester Ranger 1400 Ranger

Winchester Ranger Deer & 1400 Ranger Deer

Similar to the 1400 Ranger except: 22" or 24" cylinder bore deer barrel; rifle sights
Estimated Value: $205.00 - $260.00

Winchester Ranger & 1400 Ranger

Gauge: 12 or 20; regular or magnum
Action: Gas operated semi-automatic
Magazine: 2-shot
Barrel: 26" or 28"; Winchoke interchangeable tubes & ventilated rib
Finish: Blued; hardwood semi-pistol grip stock & forearm
Estimated Value: $200.00 - $255.00

Winchester Ranger Deer Combo

Similar to the 1400 Ranger Deer except: extra 28" ventilated rib Winchoke barrel; hardwood stock
Estimated Value: $265.00 - $330.00

Winchester 1400 Slug Hunter

Similar to the 1400 Ranger except: walnut stock and forearm; 22" barrel; improved cylinder and rifled sabot Winchoke tubes; drilled and tapped with scope base and rings; rifle sights
Estimated Value: $250.00 - $315.00

Winchester

Winchester Super X Model I

Winchester Super X Model 1 Skeet
Similar to the Super X Model 1
except: skeet stock; 26" skeet choke
barrel; ventilated rib
Estimated Value: $300.00 - $400.00

Winchester Super X Model 1 Trap
Similar to the Super X Model 1
except: regular or Monte Carlo stock;
30" full choke barrel; recoil pad
Estimated Value: $320.00 - $425.00

**Winchester Super X Model 1 &
Super X Model 1 XTR**
Gauge: 12
Action: Semi-automatic, gas operated
Magazine: 4-shot tubular
Barrel: 26"-30"; various chokes;
ventilated rib
Finish: Blued; scroll engraved alloy
receiver; checkered walnut pistol
grip stock & forearm
Estimated Value: $285.00 - $375.00

Firearms Glossary

ACP - Automatic Colt Pistol. This abbreviation is used to denote ammunition designed for semi-automatic pistols

Action - The method by which a firearm is fed ammunition and fired; the portion of the firearm responsible for feeding ammunition, firing, and extracting fired cases

Adjustable choke - A muzzle attachment, either factory or manually installed, that allows the shooter to change the choke of his shotgun; several brands are available.

AE - Automatic ejector

Autoloading - Semi-automatic action; self loading; loads cartridges into chamber using the pressure of a fired cartridge

Automatic ejector - A device for extracting the fired case from the chamber when the action is opened

Automatic safety - A safety that is put into action by reloading or cocking the fiream

Barrel - The part of a gun through which the bullet or shot passes from breech to muzzle

Barrel adapter - A device inserted into a barrel to change the gauge or caliber to a smaller size

Barrel band - A metal ring encircling the barrel and forearm, found generally on carbines, lever actions, or full length forearms

Bead - A type of sight; a small round ball on top of the barrel at the muzzle

Beavertail - Wider than average

Blowback - A semi-automatic action, this operated by the presssure of the fired cartridge

Blueing - A finishing treatment applied to the metal portions of firearms for lasting protection; named for the blue-black final appearance; minimizes light reflection and protects against rust

Bolt action - An action, either repeating or single shot, that requires manual operation of the bolt handle to feed the chamber

Glossary

Box lock - An action, with few working parts, found in break-open firearms

Box magazine - A box shaped magazine that stores and feeds the cartridges to the chamber

Breech - The rear end of the barrel where the chamber is located

Buck horn - A type of rear sight; the sides curve upward and inward over the open notch

Bull barrel - An unusually thick and heavy barrel

Butt plate - A sturdy piece attached to the rearmost section of the stock to protect the wood of the stock

Buttstock - The stock; the part of the gun extending from the receiver to the shooter's shoulder

Caliber - The diameter of the bore of a rifle or handgun

Carbine - A rifle with a short barrel, generally 16" to 20"

Case-hardened - A treatment, using carbon and extreme heat, for strengthening metal parts; the treated portion takes on a multi-coloerd, hazy finish

CB cap - A 22 caliber cartridge, shorter and less powerful than the 22 caliber short

CF (Centerfire) - A cartridge in which the primer is located in the center of the base or head

Chamber - The portion of the firearm that holds the cartridge during firing

Checkering - Patterned lines cut into the wood of grips, stocks, forearms, and slide handles; it is decorative and, at the same time, provides a non-slip surface.

Cheekpiece - An extended area in the stock used for proper cheek positioning against the stock

Choke - The design of a shotgun barrel that dictates the spread and pattern of shot leaving the barrel

Choke tube - A device that is inserted into the muzzle of a shotgun to alter the choke

Clip - A removable magazine, inserted into a firearm, that holds the cartridges and feeds them into the chamber

Comb - The upper portion of the stock

Compensator - A device attached to the muzzle or made into the barrel to reduce the upward swing of the barrel when fired

Cylinder - A rotating cartridge holder used in a revolver, in which the chambers are located

Damascus barrel - A type of barrel produced by welding small, twisted pieces of iron and steel in a spiral; these barrels were thought to be stronger in the late 1800's.

Derringer - Small, short, one or more barrelled handgun, easily concealed

Double action (DA) - Designation of a handgun that can be discharged simply by pulling the trigger; manual cocking is unneccessary

Double barrel - A gun with two barrels, lusually a shotgun, rifle, or rifle/shotgun combination with barrels side-by-side or over-and-under

Double set trigger - A device with two triggers; one sets a spring mechanism to assist the firing trigger; usually found on target guns

Dovetail - A groove by which the sight is attached to the barrel

Ejector - A mechanism for removing, or partially removing, empty cases from the gun

Exposed hammer - A visible hammer that can be manually cocked

Extractor - A device that draws the cartridge or empty case from the chamber when the actin is opened

Falling block - An action, found in some early single shots, in which the chamber closing mechanism moves vertically by moving a lever

Firing Pin - The device that strikes the primer part of a cartridge to fire the cartridges

Finish - The exterior appearance of a gun including type of wood, stock, forearm, and type of metal, sights, decoration, and added features

Fixed sights - Stationary sights; not movable

Flash supressor - An instsrument that reduces or hides muzzle flame or flash

Fluted - A shallow groove or grooves found on some forearms and on revolver cylinders

Forearm - The portion of the gun under the barrel that is gripped when firing; usually made of wood; the forearm can be in the form of a slide handle on slide action gun

Front sight - The sight at the muzzle end of the barrel

Gas operation - A type of action in which gas from a discharging cartridge is used to operate the action

Gauge - The bore size of a shotgun

Glossary

Grip safety - A safety device located on the grip of a pistol; the shooter's hand releases the safety as it grips the pistol to fire

Hammer - A spring powered piece that strikes the firing pin; it is actuated by the trigger

Hammerless - A gun with a concealed hammer or striking mechanism

Handgun - A gun that is operated with one hand; revolver, single shot, or semi-automatic pistol

Handguard - A piece that fits on top of the barrel to protect the hand from the heat of rapid fire; usually found on military type rifles

Hooded sight - A sight with a protective cover

Lanyard loop or ring - A metal ring on military handguns that is attached to a strap

Lever action - A firearm in which the action is operated by the movement of a lever, usually part of the trigger guard

Loading gate - In revolvers a piece that swings open to allow loading; in a long gun, a spring powered door that is forced open when loading cartridges into the magazine

Long - The middle designation of a 22 caliber cartridge, longer than a short, shorter than a long rifle

Long rifle - The designation of a 22 caliber cartridge; more powerful than a long

Magazine - The portion of the gun that holds cartridges ready for feeding into the chamber; in repeating weapons only

Magnum - A more powerful cartridge than the standard cartridge of the same caliber

Mannlicher stock - A one-piece stock and forearm that extends the length of the barrel

Micrometer - A highly accurate adjustable sight found mainly on target rifles or pistols

Monte Carlo - A type of stock in which there is a rise at the forward portion; usually has a cheek piece

Muzzle - Forward most end of the barrel

Open sight - A "notched" sight

Palm rest - An adjustable handgrip found on match rifles

Parkerizing - A matte, rust resistant surface applied to metal with a phosphate solution; used on military firearms

Glossary

Patridge sights - A square notched rear sight and square post front sight

Peep sight - A circular rear sight with a small hole that provides greater accuracy than open or notched sights

Pistol - Handgun; usually a semi-automatic handgun

Pistol grip - The grip portion of a handgun; or a grip resembling that of a pistol built into the stock of a shotgun or rifle

Pump - Slide action

Ramp sight - A front sight that is positioned atop a ramp base

Recoil pad - A rubber cushion attached to some shotguns and high powered rifles designed to reduce recoil impact on the shooter

Rem - Remington

Repeating - Any rifle or shotgun that has a magazine and may be fired without reloading after each shot

Revolver - A handgun that uses a rotating cylinder to hold and fire cartridges

Rib - A flat piece fitted on top of barrel to aid in sighting or add decor; may be ventilated, matte, or solid

RF (Rimfire) - A cartridge in which the firing primer is in the perimeter of the shell base or head

SAA - Single Action Army

Safety - A mechanism that prevents the gun from being fired

Schnabel - A decorative lip at the end of a forearm

Semi-automatic - An autoloading action in which cartridges are fed automatically; the trigger must be pressed for every desired discharge

Short - A small 22 caliber cartridge

Shotgun - A non-rifled long gun, designated by gauge, for firing shot shells

Side lever - A lever located on the side of a receiver that is tripped to open the gun

Single action - The hammer must be cocked before the gun can be fired

Single set trigger - A trigger that can be fired by heavy pull or put into another position to allow light pull

Pocket Guide to Shotguns

Glossary

Single trigger - A single trigger used to fire a double barrel shotgun; a selective single trigger is equipped with a lever that allows the shooter to chose the barrel to be discharged first; the non-selective trigger is always fired in the same, factory-set sequence

Slide action - A pump action long arm. An action that requires a manual slide of the forearm section (slide handle) in order to complete the action cycle

Sling - A removable strap usually attached to military, high powered hunting and some target rifles or shotguns

Snubnose - A revolver with a very short barrel

Spec. (Special) - Usually to denote ammunition (as 38 Special)

S&W - Smith & Wesson

Swivel - A metal loop through which is passed a sling for carrying; either detachable or stationary

Takedown - A gun that can be easily taken apart for transport or storage

TD - Takedown

Thumbhole - A feature found mostly on match rifles, a hole in the stock for the shooter's thumb

Thumb lever - A lever atop the frame that is tripped to break open the firearm

Thumb rest - Usually found on handgun grips, a place to rest the thumb to provide better hold

Trigger - The piece under the action that is pressed to open the firing mechanism

Trigger guard - A metal barrier around the trigger for protection of the trigger

Tubular magazine - A tube in which cartridges are stored end to end, ready to be transported to the chamber; can be under barrel or in stock

UMC - Union Metallic Cartridge Co.

Ventilated rib - A rib that is separated from the barrel by short posts

Win. - Winchester

WMR - Winchester Magnum Rim Fire

WRA - Winchester Repeating Arms Company

Pocket Guide to Shotguns

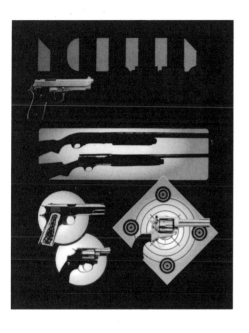

New

Schroeder's
ANTIQUES
Price Guide ... is the #1 best-selling
antiques & collectibles value guide on the market today,
and here's why . . .

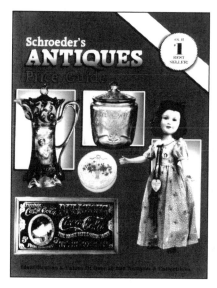

8½ X 11 • 608 Pgs. • PB • $12.95

COLLECTOR BOOKS
A Division of Schroeder Publishing Co., Inc.